"Speak softly and carry this little book around wherever you go!"

—Theodore Roosevelt

"Please read this book—it will save your reputation!"

—The Citizens of Florida

what you didn't learn
from your parents about
politics

[a guide to a polarizing subject]

matthew paul turner

and l.c. baker

TH1NK
P.O. Box 35001
Colorado Springs, Colorado 80935

ISBN-13: 9-78157683-943-0
ISBN-10: 1-57683-943-5

Cover design by Brand Navigation, LLC: DeAnna Pierce, Terra Petersen,
   and Bill Chiaravalle, www.brandnavigation.com
Cover image by CSA Images, Brandon Alms
Creative Team: Nicci Hubert, Andrea Christian, Kathy Mosier, Arvid Wallen,
   Laura Spray, Pat Reinheimer

Turner, Matthew Paul, 1973-
  What you didn't learn from your parents about politics : a guide to a
polarizing subject / Matthew Paul Turner and L.C. Baker.
     p. cm.
  Includes bibliographical references (p.   ).
  ISBN 1-57683-943-5
  1. Christian youth--Religious life--United States. 2. Christianity
and politics--United States. I. Baker, L. C. (Lisa C.) II. Title.
  BV4531.3.T88 2007
  261.70973--dc22
                              2006038390

Printed in the United States of America

1 2 3 4 5 6 7 8 9 10 / 11 10 09 08 07

FOR A FREE CATALOG OF NAVPRESS BOOKS & BIBLE STUDIES,
   CALL 1-800-366-7788 (USA) OR 1-800-839-4769 (CANADA)

Contents

Disclaimer

This book isn't a guide to being conservative. Nor is it a guide to being liberal. Though the personal stories I share about my life will certainly present a little of both views, please don't read them as an endorsement of one side or the other. I share my own stories to reflect the personal conflict over politics that people who attempt to follow Jesus often experience. It's my hope that this book will help you through your own journey.

Also, unlike the other books in this series, I've asked my friend L. C. Baker [her first name is Lisa—*she's trying so hard to be cool and literary like J. K.*] to participate with me in writing and researching this book. Without her help this book never would have been finished. And so some of her stories have found their way into the pages, though you'll always know when something was written by her.

Acknowledgments

I [Matthew Paul Turner] would like to thank:

- Jessica, my first lady
- Lisa Baker, a good writer and editor and an even better friend
- Tommy Hall: I'm blessed, bro, to have you in my corner; thank you for your friendship
- Rebekah Hubbell for friendship and guidance
- Nicci Hubert for letting me write this book, but that doesn't mean I don't hate you a little bit for moving to New York City!
- World Vision
- My editor, Andrea Christian, for helping me make this book better
- My copyeditor, Kathy Mosier, for all of your hard work on this book; it's insane how much better you make my writing
- Jackie Monahan for good PR
- And Jessica, Eric, Eric, Erin, Kent, Kate, Danielle, and everyone else at TH1NK and NavPress [don't hate me for leaving your name out]; thank you for playing a role in my book's story

And, God, if you read this book, forgive me for writing a book about politics. Please. And forgive everyone for reading it, too.

I [L. C. Baker] would like to thank:

- Matthew Paul Turner for a long friendship and for the many theological and political conversations that found their way into the book
- Dana and Brandi Bates for teaching me the importance of advocacy
- And most of all my husband, Matt, my constant source for news and political opinion, and the most supportive and encouraging spouse a writer could ever hope for

Political Jeopardy
[let's begin this book with a little trivia]

You like trivia, right? Sure, you do. So here's the question: Ann Coulter, a conservative political columnist, caused quite a stir in 2006 with her controversial title *Godless*. Can you remember what caused all the fuss?

A. Ann called the Republican Party the political voice of God Almighty.
B. Ann showed too much cleavage on the cover of *Godless*.
C. Ann suggested that Hillary Clinton was the bride of Satan.
D. Ann trashed some widows of 9/11.
E. Ann confessed in *Godless* to actually being a very slender man.

ANSWER: D. Yeah, when Matt Lauer interviewed Ann on the *Today* show, he quoted from her book: "These self-obsessed women seem genuinely unaware that 9/11 was an attack on our nation and acted as if the terrorist attack only happened to them." It went over like a lead balloon. Well, with those who have a conscience anyway. Of course, not everything Ann says is so blatantly void of compassion. But we'll get to Ann Coulter later.[1]

Introduction
[the strange and complicated world of politics]

Am I the dumbest writer in the world for trying to tackle a book about politics? I just might be. Not only am I writing a book about politics, but I'm not taking advantage of the opportunity—as most political writers do—to state my opinion about all things political in a forum where no one can contradict me. That's the great thing about writing: You get to talk without interruption, at least until the book signings and radio interviews.

But with this book, I'm really giving up some great opportunities by attempting to be open-minded about a subject that no one in his right mind would write about for any purpose other than to spout his own opinion. Before I started writing this book, my extensive research into politics [which consisted mostly of watching C-SPAN] led me to conclude that politics are all about debate. The one thing that all people who care about politics have in common is that they all get into a lot of arguments. And so I thought that the best thing I could do for my book on politics was to get a coauthor to argue with me on the page. But please don't assume from what you see here that my coauthor and I argue all the time. We don't necessarily disagree about all things political. Or even in general. And we're both nice people [most of the time]. Basically, we're just friends who get along well enough to talk about politics, which in today's world of red and blue states is kind of rare.

Anyone who writes a book about politics from an open-minded, nonpartisan, Christian perspective usually gets a fair bit of backlash—from every side. However, I think this book might make less of a splash than others, at least in some arenas. For example, I highly doubt that anyone from the Green Party will care enough about this little book to make any ill-fated remarks about it. Go Green Party!

This brings us to our first interruption. This is the coauthor, L. C. Baker. I just wanted to let you know that not everyone likes to make fun of the Green Party. I happen to think the Green Party is an excellent option to the bipartisan politics we've been experiencing lately in America. I wish third parties would gain more respect and recognition in this country; many of our worst political problems stem from the fact that we have only two viable party options – and they aren't really much different from each other. The more I study politics, the more I think issues such as environmentalism, sustainability, and localization – the core concerns of the Green Party – are the issues that have the potential to unify politicians and voters from both sides of the political spectrum. In fact, I'm a card-carrying member of the Green Party.

Okay, so maybe I'm exaggerating with that last part. But I do like the Green Party. And I have friends who are members of the Green Party. I'm pretty sure. At least one.

All right, so maybe the Green Party isn't *that* viable as a third option – at least not yet. But I did mean what I said about third parties. We could use some. But more on that later.

I was just kidding—well, about the "Go Green Party" part, not about my stupidity in writing a book about politics. That's still true.

So this book is about politics. And as you know, politics happen. Just like some other things. However, politics do serve an important and even useful purpose. But we'll get to that later.

For now, we need to ease into this conversation about all things political. I mean, there's a reason it's one of the three topics you're not supposed to bring up in front of strangers, on a first date, or in a large group. As I'm sure you're aware, politics happen in almost any area of life. There are politics at work, in family dynamics, behind closed doors at churches, in love, even in sex between husbands and wives. [Yes, there can be politics with sex. If you're married, ask your husband or wife to dress up in an Aquaman outfit and you'll probably learn a lot about the dirty politics of sex. But then again, that might be exactly what your marriage needs!]

But, you see, that's the deal when politics are involved! There's usually an angle. You can never really know the true intentions of a politician. Politics is defined as the use of tactics and strategy to gain power in a group or organization. Politics not only have the ability to control and influence governments, but they can also move and shake the emotions of people. In every situation involving politics, an individual's intentions might be for personal gain [i.e., selfish — BOO! 😠], or they might be noble [i.e., selfless — YAY! 😊]. One of the benefits of politics is having the option to either reveal your true intentions or keep them out of sight and out of mind — away from the public eye.

And so the art of politics — in love, sex, family, business, and, yes, even when running a country — can be extremely confusing. And sometimes manipulating!

But truthfully, when it comes to America's politics — um, you know, the topic of this book — the word *confusing* doesn't even begin to describe the feelings, happenings, and, yes, scandals that often occur when it comes to the governing of this land. Some might call all the hoopla of politics chaotic; others might be a bit more dramatic and call it mass mayhem; still others might think it's as awkward as Tom Cruise circa 2005 [ask Oprah]. However you describe politics — and you should feel free to use whatever adjective you want — I doubt you consider them simple. Now, you might think of politics as engaging, empowering, deplorable, or uninteresting. But you probably don't think of them as simple.

Yes, there's too much hoopla in politics for the big picture to always be understandable. However, it might come as a surprise to you but America's politics don't have to be confusing. News flash: America's system of politics—the one the Founding Fathers put into place more than two hundred years ago—is not meant to be confusing! In fact, it's relatively simple and would work fine if *people* weren't involved. [Ah, yes! The unknown X in the political equation—PEOPLE.] You see, here's the deal: When people with poor motives, overly wealthy and needy donors, and personal agendas get involved, politics become messy, confusing, and manipulative. It doesn't matter if the people involved are smart, talented, silly, wrong, right, Christian, atheist, or otherwise. And so a great deal of the time, politics seem blurry, icky, and sadly divided.

Another comment from the coauthor. While I understand Matthew's point here, I have to disagree about the source of the problem with politics. People, after all, are what politics are all about. The essence of politics is relationships – relationships among people – worked out to mutual benefit. Through politics, conflicting interests can be brought together to make something good, unifying, and beneficial for all.

But as unfortunate as the mess might sometimes seem, it's necessary for all of us to be involved in the political process, or at least to know how politics work. So come on, get involved! Our nation's prosperous future depends on it. Hey, don't laugh; it's true. Our nation is rather dependent upon people like you and me standing up for what we believe is right, true, and honorable and then trusting some politician to take what we believe to Washington DC and be our voice! [Okay, now you can laugh.] Few people know what a politician is going to do once he or she is elected. Trying to figure out what goes on inside a politician's head is pretty much an enigma, kind of like Michael Jackson's last ten years on earth, the success of Smash Mouth, and the rather abrupt aging of President Clinton. Yet that's how America works, and I don't see that changing in the foreseeable future.

But that whole "standing up" thing I just mentioned is another reason politics can become quite confusing and chaotic. Here's the deal: What you believe to be right, true, and honorable might be very different from what I believe is right, true, and honorable. And both of us have every right to speak our minds in this country [one of the great freedoms we have in America]!

Using your voice is a good thing. And understanding the political process and how it works will only help make your voice stronger and more effective. That's one of the reasons I've written *What You Didn't Learn from Your Parents About Politics*: I'm hoping it will help you make some kind of sense out of the mystery of politics and will encourage you to not take lightly your role, your voice, and your right as an American citizen to let your opinions be heard—and to do so effectively.

Okay, so I'm beginning to sound like a politician—you know, combining rhetoric and inspiration with the language of a third grader. But please, *you* try writing a book about politics in a way that is nonpartisan [which might be an enigma of its own] and see if you can do it without sounding a wee bit like a politician. [I'm Matthew Paul Turner, and I approve this message!]

Now, for people who follow Jesus, there tends to be another barrel of confusion when thinking about politics. Mainly, it's a question of how our faith should interact with our politics, something we'll be talking about throughout this book.

Personally Speaking . . .

For me, there was a time in the not-so-distant past when I knew exactly where I stood on most political issues. Because I was an evangelical Christian, I thought my political views had to mirror exactly what I heard being preached from the pulpit [yes, politics in the pulpit—can you believe it?], articulated over Christian radio [God save Janet Parshall!], and written in Christian books [yes, James Dobson writes books]. Despite that often cumbersome law that separates church from state—and sometimes seems as real in our modern culture as Joan Rivers' face—the church I attended as a kid always seemed to equate godly with the Republican Party. The pastor always prefaced his support of Republicans by saying, "Now, I'm not telling you who to vote for, but I'm going to vote for the candidate who is currently president. . . . But don't let that influence you. . . ."

Some might think that being Christian should make politics simpler, but often it complicates it even more. However, despite the often strange dynamics that ensue when Christianity and politics get in the same Washington DC room for cocktails—nonalcoholic, of course—it is indeed possible for faith to be integrated into our personal politics without surrendering our personal integrity to one side of the political aisle or the other. But for quite some time, I didn't think that was possible. But perhaps that's because I was pretty much molded into a right-wing conservative before I had pubic hair.

By the time I was twelve years old, you might have considered me a young George W. Bush. [Instead of W, you would have called me P.] As a preteen, I already understood the basic aspects of the political process, watched the most important

campaigns closely, and knew exactly who I would vote for and, just as important, why. Back then, I thought selling your soul to the GOP [Grand Old Party] was the Christian thing to do. I knew early on that when I turned eighteen, I'd support the elephants.

My cordial relationship with politics began in sixth grade. That's the year I thoroughly began aligning myself with the Christian conservative platform. It might sound completely ridiculous for a twelve-year-old to be this interested in politics, but I was uncoordinated and so playing sports wasn't necessarily an option for me. My love affair with politics started as I watched the 1984 election between Ronald Reagan and Walter Mondale. Something lit a spark in me. That election day, I sat at home with a notebook in hand and watched ABC's *World News Tonight* with Peter Jennings [recording every comment said and the exact moments when state results were announced]. It was clear early on in the evening that Mr. Reagan was going to win the election with a certain amount of ease. But for some reason—maybe it was ABC's cool red and blue maps or the heart-pounding music that was played each time a state's results were announced, or maybe it was the passion each and every person Peter Jennings interviewed possessed for the political process—that night watching The Gipper [a nickname for Ronald Reagan] slaughter [politically speaking, of course] Walter Mondale [and it was a slaughter: 525 electoral votes to 13] made me fall in love with politics.

My sixth grade teacher at the Christian school I attended couldn't keep his political leanings out of his lectures. He'd convinced me and all of the other students that if Walter Mondale were to become president of the United States,

America would more than likely become a communist country, just like the USSR, China, or Canada. [It wasn't until a little later that I learned Canada wasn't actually a communist country; however, my teacher was not convinced.] Like the majority of people in America, Mr. Kustings had an uncanny love and admiration for Ronald Reagan, and sometimes, like so many who love politics do, he went a little overboard with his political antics. When I arrived for class the next morning, there was a huge sign on the blackboard that said, "Hallelujah! Reagan Wins the Election!"

Home life and politics were indeed mixed in the Turner house, but only on occasion [usually around the presidential elections]. My mom and dad were Reagan Democrats, which is a term political commentators used to describe working-class Democratic Americans who in 1980 and 1984 [and some in 1988] crossed party lines to vote for the Republican candidate. Though the majority of people considered to be Reagan Democrats voted for Reagan because of his strong stance on national security and his promise to lower taxes, in 1980  [Reagan's first election] Mom and Dad were relatively new Christians, and that election was the first time their faith played a significant role in who they supported. Having registered as Democrats twenty years before when Dad said the Democratic Party stood for legislation and values that were more in line with their personal ideals, they kept their Democrat registration, but they've voted straight-ticket Republican since 1980. Though my mom and dad would never have considered themselves to be political activists, they certainly involved themselves in the political process and encouraged me to do the same. And of course their influence played a significant role in my political belief system until the early part of my adulthood. [While their influence is still invaluable to me, we learned a few years ago that we don't agree on everything. And besides, this book is about what you — and I — *didn't* learn from our parents.]

When it came to learning the ins and outs of politics, being raised in a Christian environment

she did star in *The Quick and the Dead*. Yeah, and she might be able to do it while wearing stiletto heels! Hot!

* Though we would never have wanted to cuddle with President Theodore Roosevelt, somebody must have thought he was fuzzy, warm, and, uh, cuddly, because the traditional teddy bear was named for him![2]

* Um, so yeah, we think being a part of the Kennedy clan may have a few privileges. [Of course, they seem to have tragedy, too.] When John F. Kennedy was twenty-one years old, his daddy gave him one million dollars. Yeah, daddy Kennedy was so rich that he gave each of his nine kids a mil when they turned twenty-one.[3]

[which of course included home, church, school, friends, and entertainment] was both good and bad. On one hand I learned the importance of my faith playing an active role in the political process, but on the other hand, I learned to view the political system in America much like I viewed Luke Skywalker and Darth Vader: There was a good side [for me, that was the Republican Party] and there was a dark, evil side [which, for me, was the Democratic Party]. It was always us versus them. I was raised to believe that if America ever allowed the bad side to have control, there would be doom and gloom. Heck, some even thought a Democratic president would bring on the apocalypse. Perhaps you experienced a similar upbringing; of course, for you, the "good" and the "bad" sides might have been switched, but you get the point.

When we are young, a lot can influence our view of politics — our economic situation, whether or not church or religion plays a significant role in our lives, our education, even the part of the country we live in. But perhaps the most important influence comes from our moms and dads. That's right: Parents do play a significant role in helping us form our initial political opinions. Consider these quotes from twentysomethings who talk about how their parents influenced their politics:

- "When I was eighteen, I was pretty much a young version of my outspoken father. Dad was very opinionated; it wasn't until I was well into my college education that I began to do a little thinking for myself. . . . Dad thought I'd gone off the deep end." *Daniel, 24*

- "My parents were extremely influential in helping me shape my views on issues that often get thrown into the political debate, i.e., abortion, gay marriage, prayer in schools, and the freedom of speech." *Marti, 23*

- [Laughs] "Well, my parents weren't really involved in politics—I mean, Mom was always pro gun control, but that was about it. . . . I don't think about politics all that much; I probably should." *Zach, 21*

- "Mom and Dad were hippies who became Christians in the seventies. However, they didn't base their political opinions on two or three issues. They were defenders of the environment long before it was considered posh; they stayed almost exclusively Democratic because they felt Jesus would have cared about people like the homeless and the poor. I've definitely followed in my mom and dad's footsteps." *Kaci, 28*

All of the twentysomethings I interviewed said their parents had a profound influence on their conservative, moderate, liberal, or indifferent political view. Some said their parents were so exclusively one-sided that it turned them off from politics altogether. Others said their parents' passions inspired them to be involved in politics. Many said that on one occasion or another they thought their parents' methodology wasn't always correct or that their moms and dads had too much of an us-versus-them mind-set.

It's of utmost importance that Christians [and non-Christians, too], regardless of the political party they think they adhere to, become informed on how America's politics works. And furthermore, it's imperative that we know not only how this country functions politically but also how God views politics, the issues, and, most importantly, how a heart devoted to pursuing faith in Jesus should respond to the governing of this country and the creating of policy.

I hope this book helps you engage the topic of politics, but please keep in mind: This book will help you only if it's combined with a little wisdom, grace, a mouth guard, rock-hard abs [kidding, of course], prayer, and a MacBook Pro.

So, yeah, here's to learning what you didn't learn from your parents about politics.

Enjoy,

Matthew
[and yes, J. K., I mean, L. C.]
matthew@dottedline.net
www.

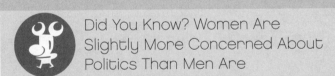

Did You Know? Women Are Slightly More Concerned About Politics Than Men Are

In the 2004 presidential election, 74 percent of women and 71 percent of men registered to vote. Yet only 65 percent of women who registered actually voted, compared to 62 percent of registered men. Historically, men have usually been more into voting than women have been [partly because women weren't allowed to vote until 1920]; however, that began to change in 1984 when, for the first time, a higher percentage of women voted than men.[4]

You might not know this, but your mom has a lot to do with how you think about politics. Now, there's no data to prove this theory, but I think after you read this sidebar, you will most certainly agree.

Okay, so when it comes to politics, you describe yourself like this . . .	Your mama's all-time favorite politician probably is . . .	In 2000, your mama most-likely voted for . . .	More than likely, your mama's idea of Satan is . . .
Flaming right-wing conservative.	Ronald Reagan, but she's harbored a secret crush on W since the early eighties.	George W. Bush, of course. And she thought Al Gore was a big fat crybaby for demanding a Florida recount.	Ted Kennedy. [Actually, she probably hates all of Massachusetts, too.]
Highly irritable left-wing liberal.	Bill Clinton, but every time she thinks about Al Franken, her Democratic heart begins to pitter-patter.	Um, Al Gore. She still thinks naughty thoughts every time Katherine Harris comes to mind.	Dick Cheney. Of course, she sometimes likes to call him simply by his first name. [And she can't stand Libby Dole, but that's just because she hates the name Libby.]
Um, pretty much clueless about politics.	Oprah! [Long live the queen!]	Whichever candidate she thought looked kinder.	The neighbor down the street who hasn't returned the garden hose she borrowed two weeks ago.
Independent, baby!	Well, it all depends on the mood she's in come election day: In 1980, she liked Reagan. In 1992, she liked Bill Clinton.	She flipped a coin because she couldn't decide between the lesser of the two "evils."	Government. And ABC when it canceled My So-Called Life and Thirtysomething.

Okay, so when it comes to politics, you describe yourself like this...	When you turned eighteen, she might have given you this advice ...	If she were to run for president, her platform would probably include ...	There's a good chance you've heard your mama say this ...
Flaming right-wing conservative.	"Please don't ever tell me if you vote for a Democrat."	National Causation Day! [*Of course, National Quilt-Making Day would be a close second.*]	"Michael Moore can burn in hell as far as I'm concerned. . . . No, really, he can. And he probably will."
Highly irritable left-wing liberal.	"Remember, baby, God is neither Republican nor Democrat, but he most definitely likes us better."	Earth Day EVERY day! [*Of course, she'd also do away with our military, which would leave America feeling a little naked.*]	"Who cares if Michael Moore is a fat man? He makes me swoon."
Um, pretty much clueless about politics.	"Honey, you should really learn how to sew a button on a shirt."	Scrapbooking!	"Bless her heart." [*Which, of course, means she's as dumb as a brick.*]
Independent, baby!	"Go on a tour of Europe, baby! I'll pay for it."	We'd all become Canadians!	"Jesus heals the soul eternally, but Guinness is sometimes a nice foretaste of that coming glory."

Truth to Know

Attention, all! See the marvels of God!
    He plants flowers and trees all over the
        earth,
Bans war from pole to pole,
    breaks all the weapons across his knee.
"Step out of the traffic! Take a long,
    loving look at me, your High God,
    above politics, above everything."

(Psalm 46:8-10)

For years, music has been a vital way for political activists to get their views out into the public arena. Not familiar with government supporting or bashing set to a catchy beat? Well, think Willie Nelson, Bob Dylan, The Rolling Stones, Janis Joplin, Nirvana, and Michael Jackson. Political tunes have covered everything from war to sexual orientation to flag burning. And this kind of music can be either pro all of these things or anti, depending on the artist, our country's current political temperature, and the topic at hand. For your listening pleasure, here are ten twenty-first-century songs that protest life as we know it or as the artist saw it.

Song	Artist	Topic[s]	What made the song controversial
"American Idiot"	Green Day	War, gay rights	Green Day pretty much insults everyone in this song.
"A King & a Kingdom"	Derek Webb	Faith, patriotism, social activism	Mr. Webb sings about seeing the kingdom in the everyday.
"Courtesy of the Red, White and Blue (The Angry American)"	Toby Keith	America	Oh, he sings about America being totally bad-a** and kicking people if they disagree with us.
"Millennium Theater"	Ani DiFranco	Terrorism, media, the Middle East, the environment	Well, Ani sings of melting ice caps and a ruined New Orleans in this not-so-subtle tune.

Song	Artist	Topic[s]	What made the song controversial
"American Life"	Madonna	America, President Bush, materialism [I love when Madonna sings against materialism — it's the greatest of contradictions.]	The material girl sings passionately about not being materialistic.
"All That We Let In"	Indigo Girls	War, death	Words about war have never sounded so harmonizing.
"Youth of a Nation"	P.O.D.	Violence, children, suicide	P.O.D. sings about violence in the inner cities.
"Not Ready to Make Nice"	Dixie Chicks	Censorship	The Chicks sing about getting an angry letter just because they spoke their minds.
"World on Fire"	Sarah McLachlan	Poverty, world hunger, 9/11, social activism	Sarah thinks the world is going to hell in a handbasket.
"This Ain't No Rag, It's a Flag"	Charlie Daniels Band	America	There's nothing like a country song that rhymes run with the word gun.

What You Need to Know About the Basics of Politics in America

[all the good, bad, and hoopla that gave us our current rules regarding politics]

Politicians are like diapers. They both need changing regularly, and for the same reason.

— Anonymous

WELCOME TO SECTION 1!

Okay, so before we begin talking about the basics of politics in America, let's get one thing straight: You are one lucky individual for having picked up *this* book about politics instead of one of the hundreds of books available in bookstores. Because if you were reading any of the other books that attempt to educate you about America's politics, you'd probably become quite bored with the mundane fascination with history, lengthy attention to detail, and downright snobbery of the authors. But since you're reading this book, you'll get all the basics that you really need to know—without any of the big words that most college-educated people don't even understand.

★ ★ ★ ★ ★ ★ ★ ★ ★ ★ ★ ★ ★ ★ ★ ★ ★

L. C. Baker again. Sorry, but I just have to get this off my chest. What is it with Turner and his distaste for big words? True, Strunk and White recommend in *Elements of Style* [the grammar and style bible for all good writers] that writers always use the shortest word that will suffice for their meaning. But some issues in politics are complicated. Yes, we'll try to make this book simple and easy to understand, but we're not going to be afraid to tackle hard issues, either. And if that means the book needs to be a little intellectual, well, you can handle that, can't you? Of course you can. At least I hope you can, because if you're reading this book, then you're probably an American citizen and a voter, which means that my political future – and Turner's and everyone else's in this country – is, at least in some small part, in your hands. So I hope you're intelligent enough to handle it.

Because if not, then maybe it's time we forget about this whole democracy idea and think about switching to an oligarchy of the intelligentsia. [There! I just used *two* words of more than three syllables in one breath! Take that, Matthew Paul Turner!]

And on top of that, you won't find the political slant that most books about politics contain. Now, that's not to say this book is silly and without opinion [i.e., imagine if Jessica Simpson were a book]; it's just that as a writer, a human being, and an American citizen, I think I have a pretty good idea of what interests most Americans. And no, I'm not talking about sex. Hello? This is a Christian book, which of course means no nudity is allowed within its pages! No Christian books are allowed to have naked flesh graze their pages. So it's indeed impossible for this book to contain any nakedness. [Well, I guess you could strip off your clothes, open to page 112, and sit on it, but that's certainly the only way nudity would get on any page of this book.] But as I was saying, most Americans want the bottom line, the gist of the topic without needless information, and they want to have a little fun while they read. And I can promise that at least two out of three of those needs will be met with this book. [I can't really claim that writing a book without some needless information is necessarily my greatest literary gift.]

The Editors Present: Other Types of Governments America Could Have Had but Thankfully Avoided!

Hello again, it's the editors! As you know, America's government is a form of democracy! Most Americans LOVE being a part of our kind of democracy. [Now, some right-leaning individuals think liberals hate it, but that's up for debate.] Some Americans like democracy so much that they go spreading our form of it all over the world, or at least they try to. [BTW: If you know of any countries interested in America's form of democracy — which includes freedom, liberty, and if you're really lucky, some not too shabby health care — you might have them call the president; it's our understanding that the U.S. government is quite open to helping other countries get started on their personal path toward democracy!]

Anyway, we thought it might behoove you to know what other types of government are out there; heck, if nothing else, it might give you a better appreciation for democracy!

	Totalitarian	Theocracy
Led by . . .	One man, who is usually not very nice and for some reason has really bad teeth.	God, or that country's "idea" of God, which could very well mean it's not the "real" God.
You're allowed to . . .	Say nice things about the leaders, like, "I love him!" and "He's the best!"	Follow a cloud by day and a burst of fire by night, but not the other way around!
You're not allowed to . . .	Talk to foreign media!	Eat shrimp!
On Friday evenings, you . . .	Pray that the mean man who leads your country will die a miserable death, but you just don't tell anyone.	Wander around in the wilderness. And you probably feel like you've been wandering for years.
One country that adheres to this form of government is . . .	Cuba.	Biblical Israel.
Ronald Reagan might say . . .	"Hmm, the facts are stubborn things, aren't they?"	Ronald Reagan refused to comment — we're sorry for any inconvenience this may have caused.

	Socialist state [or Socialist republic]	Constitutional monarchy	Robertsonism
Led by . . .	Mr. Government.	An elected prime minister who works under the limitations and freedoms of a constitution.	Pat Robertson and his son!
You're allowed to . . .	Choose your own grapefruits at the corner market, and sometimes you get candy.	Do anything you want as long as you're not pissing off Prince William or Prince Harry.	Donate money to his small country in Virginia! And you can make sneering remarks about other country's leaders!
You're not allowed to . . .	Climb over the large barbed-wire fence that surrounds your country!	See Her Majesty the Queen, and if you do, close your eyes!	Vote Democrat!
On Friday evenings, you . . .	Eat grapefruit and devise a plan to get over that blasted barbed-wire fence.	Sleep around!	Watch TiVo'd episodes of The 700 Club.
One country that adheres to this form of government is . . .	China.	The United Kingdom.	Parts of Colorado Springs.
Ronald Reagen might say . . .	"I was wondering if you had any Peking chicken?"	"Make my day! No really, get over here and make my day, Margaret Thatcher, you hot little dickens."	"Mr. Robertson, tear down this wall!"

However, back to my original point: You really are lucky to be reading this book! So without further boasting, I'll just get started on the basics of politics, and I'll try to leave out all the needless information I just referred to. At least mostly.

American History
[a quick overview]

First things first!
We are governed by a democracy.
[well, sort of]

I'm not sure why most of us so quickly forget everything we learned in our high school history classes. But we do. And consequently, we forget important little pieces of information like the fact that America isn't a pure democracy. Now, as I'm quite sure you've heard on an occasion or two, democracy is simply people ruling [or governing] themselves. But America's type of governing is a form of democracy, not a 100 percent democracy. We only have to think back to the 2000 election in order to remember that—Al Gore won the popular vote, but George W. Bush was still elected president. But we'll get to all that not-a-true-democracy stuff in a second. But first, we interrupt this boring paragraph with a couple of interesting ones about America's early settlers.

The early birds get the worms.

[and chase away the Native Americans]

I think it's important for us to understand that America's type of government was unique in the seventeenth and eighteenth centuries. Those who settled here in America were looking for something new; most of them didn't want to travel all the way across the Atlantic just to find the same political nightmare they left behind in England.

When the Pilgrims came over from England, I'm not sure they knew what they were getting themselves into. Sure, the one hundred or so of them wanted to worship God without having to tell King James what they were doing. Of course, the holy clan had quite a few reasons for being anti-England [in addition to being anti-England, they were also anti-fans of the colors pink, yellow, Kelly green, and baby blue. Pastels were obviously of the Devil]. However, considering that the Pilgrims were rather private individuals, I don't think they necessarily expected their departure to start a trend of ticked-off religious Englishmen boarding ships for America in hopes of finding things like the freedom to worship God the way they darn well pleased and the freedom to say things like, "The king of England smells like poo" and "He's a big fat stinky head" in the public square.

Other Parties!

Though most in America belong to the Democratic or Republican Parties, there are other more obscure political parties that you might find interesting. Or you might think they're dumb, but hey, the small parties are a part of politics, too. So here are a few:

❋ *The Alaskan Independence Party.* A small political party in Alaska whose adherents think the big, cold state to our north should secede from the rest of the country. They're ticked they didn't get the chance eighty years ago. And I've heard it isn't cool to mess with an angry Alaskan. [*Free Alaska!*]

❋ *American Nazi Party.* Huh. I'm pretty sure the members of this party are all bound for hell. But I guess I can't be sure, even with Nazis. [*Is it wrong for me to not care?*]

❋ *Communist Party.* No political makeup would be complete without the Commies! [*CCCP!*]

❋ *Marijuana Party.* You can probably guess what this party stands for; yep, they want to bring an end to the war on

But the trend did begin. People began to pour into America's spacious skies [okay, no, they didn't actually live in the skies; I was just trying to reference "America the Beautiful"].

Yet the men and women who ventured to America's shore weren't simply running away from their mother country; they had vision for the future! They wanted to chart new territory, bring about a new type of government in the world, build really big buildings, and, by golly, not have body odor. [*Unfortunately for the early American colonists, Procter & Gamble didn't come about until much later.*]

In 1776, we got our freedom.

[of course, this was more than 150 years after the Pilgrims landed at Plymouth Rock]

Thank God for people like Thomas Jefferson, George Washington, Patrick Henry, and Benjamin Franklin. It was due to the strength and determination of men like these [apparently women were home cooking stew, raising their twenty-seven kids, scrapbooking, and sewing flags] that America eventually became its own entity, one nation under God, a more perfect union, and the "greatest country in the known world." Yeah, you know what I'm talking about, right? [*Of course, it wasn't until years later that Americans thought they were completely bad-a**.*]

drugs, which I guess is the same thing most of us want, really.

✳*New Party.* Apparently, this party is in harsh opposition to the *old* party. And guess what? The New Party doesn't exist anymore, making them the old New Party.

✳*The Workers Party.* A self-described left-wing party that stands for anti-imperialism and anticapitalism.

A Random Act of Trivia

QUESTION: What hard-hitting journalist [with great legs] is the CBS news anchor?

A. Katie "I miss *Today*" Couric
B. Katie "I talk about my daughters way too much" Couric
C. Katie "eat your heart out, Charles Gibson" Couric
D. Katie "Republicans make me sick to my stomach" Couric

ANSWER: Um, well, this one is up to you!

Seven Things You Should Know About America's Political Beginnings

1. In 1776, Thomas Jefferson's Declaration of Independence accomplished three things:

   ❂ Established a new theory of government. [The old theory included a king, a queen, and another king's lover.]

   ❂ Listed a slew of reasons America needed to be divided from England's brash form of monarchy. [Which included the freedom to have ice in all McDonald's drinks!]

✪ ✪ ✪ ✪ ✪ ✪ ✪ ✪ ✪ ✪ ✪ ✪ ✪ ✪ ✪ ✪ ✪ ✪ ✪

This is the coauthor – *again*! I really don't mean to be argumentative, but hey, that's what I'm here for. I just wanted to point out that some of these "facts," like most facts in history, could be debated. For instance, the Declaration of Independence and later the Constitution didn't necessarily establish a new theory of government. The Constitution was based on theories that had been developed by European philosophers such as John Locke [whose idea of government as a "social contract" led to the Constitutional phrase about the government "deriving their just powers from the consent of the governed"] and Baron de Montesquieu [who came up with the idea of separation of powers within government]. What was unique about the Constitution is that it was the first time those aesthetic theories were actually put into practice in a working government. Obviously they worked pretty well because today the Constitution is the oldest government document in the world, and in two hundred years, we've made only twenty-seven corrections in the form of amendments.

✪ ✪ ✪ ✪ ✪ ✪ ✪ ✪ ✪ ✪ ✪ ✪ ✪ ✪ ✪ ✪ ✪ ✪ ✪

   ❂ Declared war on those bloody redcoats! [And it's a shame, too; those red coats were hot!]

   ❂ BONUS POINT: This document also made it clear that Mr. Jefferson had impeccable handwriting!

2 Not everyone was so sure America should break away from England. In fact, for many, the War of Independence was not a war for independence at all; it was simply a war against the unjust laws of England. [Little did they know that Jefferson had other things in mind—like fireworks, hotdogs with mustard, and kickball!]

3 In March of 1781, The Articles of Confederation was ratified, which was the first official document binding America's states together as one. But it didn't include one currency that was used across all states.

4 Early Americans didn't agree on everything [much like today's Americans!]. The early battles included these things:

- ☸ The legalization of slavery. [The Northern states didn't want it—YAY! 🙂 The Southern states did—BOO! 🙁]

- ☸ Equal representation for BIG states and small states. [Which eventually led to America becoming a democratic republic and not a pure democracy.]

- ☸ Oh, and Maryland and Virginia were constantly arguing over their property line! [Um, so mature!]

5 In May of 1787, representatives from twelve of the thirteen states [fifty-five in all] met in Philadelphia to make plans for a new document of government—this is known as the

Constitutional Convention! [The folks from Rhode Island had a stick up their behinds and so they tried overcompensating for their state's small size by refusing to send anyone to the BIG meeting.]

During the course of the summer of 1787, those representatives met to discuss how our country would govern itself. After two plans were presented [one from Virginia, a large state, and one from New Jersey, a small state], they eventually decided on a compromise [in fact, it was called The Great Compromise]. This led to the Constitution of the United States, in which the following decisions were made:

- Three branches of government would exist: the executive branch, the legislative branch, and the judicial branch. [We'll talk about the executive branch in a bit!]
- Each state would receive two forms of representation [i.e., two congressional houses]: In one, a state's number of representatives would be based on the state's population, and in the other, each state would have exactly two representatives without regard to the population.
- The judicial branch would be the only branch in which members would be voted into office for life or until they decided to retire.
- The right to choose these representatives — the president and the members of the two forms of Congress — was ultimately given to the people. [Between you and me, rumor has it that this group of men meeting in Philadelphia thought the average person was dumb and uninformed! So I guess we should consider ourselves lucky that we're allowed to have a say!]

7 When the Constitution was taken back to the individual states, some pretty extensive disagreements broke out between the Federalists and the Anti-Federalists! [Original, huh!] And politics ensued! People on both sides ran ads, wrote papers, and distributed their point of view among the common folk. Still, the Constitution passed—though in some states, it was quite close!

L. C. Baker again. It's a funny thing how issues we thought were resolved hundreds of years ago still resurface in politics today. You don't hear about it much — another example of the bias in our understanding of history and politics — but the Anti-Federalist movement never really died out completely. True, the states ratified the Federalist government, and when the Southern Confederacy lost the Civil War, it was pretty well established that the United States was, well, united. From then on, it appeared everybody was in agreement that we'd all be one big happy family. But think again. Though it has yet to be a significant issue in any modern political election, secessionism is still alive and well as a movement — if a little, well, small. It's strongest in the Pacific Northwest, where a few secessionists hope to establish the Republic of Cascadia by combining the states of Oregon and Washington [and maybe northern California and southern Alaska] with the Canadian province of British Columbia. It's hard in today's day and age to even imagine the United States ever breaking apart. But there was that bit about the red and blue states [you know, the election map of 2000 and 2004], which might have indicated a cultural divide greater than we have yet realized. And, of course, despite having lost the war a long time ago, there are certainly plenty of hopefuls in the South who would gladly take the opportunity to rise again if they thought Cascadia would ally with them in a second attempt.[1]

A Special Bonus Section Featuring the Editors!!!
[get to know the Founding Fathers!]

Hello, politics fans! Are we allowed to call you politics fans? I mean, we know there's a decent chance you're not huge fans of all this stuff, but we figure if you've made it this far, you're at least having some fun. Because we're the editors of this book, we get to make changes whenever we want. And let's face it: Matthew and what's-her-name—oh, L. C. Baker [*Who does she think she is? J. K.?*]—have been great throughout this book, but we feel there needs to be a little pick-me-up before we get into the three branches of government. [I mean, how exciting can they be?]

So we decided to add some fun featuring our Founding Fathers! [*F, F, F, and F. How's that for alliteration?*] As you know, when it comes to the combo of Christianity and politics here in America, there's always been a lot of talk about the deep Christian faith of our Founding Fathers. So it's a must for any book about politics [*especially a Christian book*] to have at least a few pages dedicated to those great God-fearing men and women [well, *men*, anyway] who helped make it possible for America to have churches on every street corner, Christian T-shirts, and Third Day! [*What would we do without Third Day?*] Without the faith-filled determination of these men, we might be listening to enlightenment music or, worse, *transcendental* music [*which we're sure would all sound like Björk*]. Anyway, lucky for us, the Founding Fathers were all evangelicals [*well, they really weren't, but please don't tell James Dobson we said that—we don't like to see grown men cry, and we don't want to get the Grand Evangelical Pooh-Bah on our bad side!*] because if they hadn't been, we wouldn't have W! [*Um, we're just being silly!*] Anyway, without further ado, let's get started!

[BTW: VOTE FOR THE EDITORS IN 2020!!!! WE MIGHT RUN FOR PRESIDENT.]

SAY HELLO TO GEORGE WASHINGTON!

[gosh, he could have really used some twenty-first-century hair product, couldn't he?]

[1732–1799]

His **hands** are kind of chunky, huh? And they look rather soft, too. [*We want to know what skin conditioner he used!*] But these are the hands that held the Bible when George was having his quiet times with God.

Okay, so we've learned that our first president was known for his calm, soothing nature; in fact, it's said that George's faith kept everything in his life unruffled except **his shirts**. His fashion is *so Marilyn Manson* — though pretty much all the Founding Fathers dressed a bit goth!

Now, you can't tell from looking at his **sad, thin lips**, but George was actually a happy sort of fellow. And wise, too! From these lips came the words, "Observe good faith and justice toward all nations. Cultivate peace and harmony with all." Yes, we know quite a few politicians in today's world who could learn a thing or two from Mr. Washington's *faith in action!*

Well, it looks as if Fred from *Scooby Doo* wasn't the first to make the ascot look rather dashing. Every time George went to church [which according to the 1936 book *The Religious Beliefs of Our Presidents*, Washington rarely attended church — and when he did, he didn't take Communion]. [2] But when he did go, you can be sure he wore **an ascot**. Eighteenth-century fashionable correctness was incomplete without one!

One thing you may not know about him: He had dentures made of ivory and animal's teeth, but by gosh, he still flossed!

If alive today, he'd be: At the dentist!

Best known for: Being America's first president and marrying Martha!

Not known for: Speaking. His false teeth made that difficult!

Fashionably aware? Well, would you consider a man with dog's teeth runway material?

WWJD? Give him some new teeth!

Most controversial moment: He was a horrible speller. [That's true!]

Worth quoting? "It is better to offer no excuse than a bad one."

A NICELY WIGGED JOHN ADAMS

[is he wearing
a bow?]

[1735–1826]

The only thing tighter than John's curls was the bond with God that kept him on the straight and narrow.

What is this? Is it a growth? Speaking of growth, did I mention that John pursued a great deal of spiritual growth throughout his life?

Of all the presidents, John had the best eyebrows! I think he must have waxed. Of course, this has nothing to do with his Christianity, unless his eyebrow fetish has something to do with being in the Christian rock band the Newsboys. [Black tattooed eyeliner not included.]

His double chin is further proof that he was most definitely a Christian.

One thing you may not know about him: He got into a tiff with Jefferson and actually pulled the Jesus card!

If alive today, he'd be: A guest on *The 700 Club*!

Best known for: Being America's second president!

Not known for: Good hair. *The poor guy possibly had the worst case of male pattern baldness we've ever seen!*

Fashionably aware? Heck yeah! He single-handedly resurrected the use of crushed velvet!

WWJD? Teach him to be a happy loser!

Most controversial moment: He was the first to use mudslinging.

Worth quoting? "I must study politics and war that my sons may have liberty to study mathematics and philosophy."

THOMAS JEFFERSON, THE ORIGINAL DEMOCRAT

[and one who probably
wouldn't get along with
Jesse Jackson]

[1743–1826]

Poofy hair might imply he was a fan of twentieth-century church fashion; either that or he just saw the ghost of Jonathan Edwards.

Jerry Falwell's a fan! He said, "Jefferson is a man whom I hold in high regard, and I would have supported his efforts to disestablish the Anglican Church if I had been one of his contemporaries."[3] Jerry supports anyone in favor of bringing down a liberal church!

The perfectly ruffled scarf around his neck implies . . . well, I'll let you decide what it implies.

Jefferson said, "I'm a great believer in luck, and I find the harder I work the more I have of it." Wait a minute, Christians don't believe in luck!

One thing you may not know about him: T. J. loved houseplants! He had a collection.

🐚 🐚 🐚

If alive today, he'd be: Just like Hillary! [*Please send all hate mail directly to Matthew!*]

🐚 🐚 🐚

Best known for: The Declaration of Independence and being our third president.

🐚 🐚 🐚

Not known for: Loving peaches, but he did! He had 160 peach trees!

🐚 🐚 🐚

Fashionably aware? Absolutely! He was our nation's very first metrosexual!

🐚 🐚 🐚

WWJD? Heal him!

🐚 🐚 🐚

Most controversial moment: It's rumored that he slept around with his slaves.

🐚 🐚 🐚

Worth quoting? "A democracy is nothing more than mob rule, where fifty-one percent of the people may take away the rights of the other forty-nine."

BEN FRANKLIN, HE'S OUR MAN! IF HE CAN'T DO IT, NO ONE CAN!

[of course, he'll more than likely need a kite]

[1706–1790]

Oh my gosh, that's a collar! For a second, I thought Ben had a Southern gospel singer wrapped around his neck.

Yes, we know Ben looks a bit dazed and confused in this picture, but we promise you he was a very happy man. Now, his happiness didn't necessarily come from his personal relationship with Jesus Christ; he basically practiced healthy living. But did we mention that it doesn't seem his healthy living included a diet? In fact, he looks a little constipated.

Wit and wisdom is what Ben did best. Now, like I mentioned in What You Didn't Learn from Your Parents About Money, most of Ben's wisdom was ever so slightly influenced by the book of Proverbs. You see, our Ben was raised an Episcopalian and therefore he was quite learned in biblical studies. So it's not out of the question to suggest that he ripped off Solomon quite a bit — and without attribution.

One thing you may not know about him: He was quite good with the ladies. . . . I mean, he *did* discover electricity.

If alive today, he'd be: Rich.

Best known for: Witty sayings that make even the purest humans feel like BIG FAT sinners.

Not known for: Late nights and sleeping in.

Fashionably aware? Is electricity sexy? How about saving money?

WWJD? Ask him for advice? [Nah, we're just kidding!]

Most controversial moment: Dying.

Worth quoting? "Eat to live and not live to eat."

Did you know that the United States Constitution is the oldest enduring written national constitution? That's pretty cool! That means America has always attempted to stay on its original course as a single united entity. Now, some would argue that. But despite all the naysayers, the Constitution protects YOU! It's an important document that you should know something about.

⇨ **When was the Constitution written?** 1787. [Of course, some say it's been rewritten since then, but not really!] It was created in what is known today as Independence Hall in Philadelphia, the same place the Declaration of Independence was signed!

⇨ **When did the Constitution become official?** It wasn't approved by the necessary nine of twelve states until June 1788. Delaware was the first state to jump on board — that's why they have "First State" on their license plate! New Hampshire was the ninth state to join in the fun.

⇨ **What is the Preamble to the Constitution?** Well, the Preamble is simply an intro. And those who wrote the Constitution didn't waste words; it's very short for being the introduction to the most important national document! Here it is in its entirety: "We the People of the United States, in Order to form a more perfect Union, establish Justice, insure domestic Tranquility, provide for the common defense, promote the general Welfare, and secure the Blessings of Liberty to ourselves and our Posterity, do ordain and establish this Constitution for the United States of America."

⇨ **What is the Bill of Rights?** In 1791, some of the original framers and state delegates decided that the Constitution needed to include individuals' rights! James Madison stepped up to the plate and proposed ten changes [or amendments] to the Constitution — including the freedom of speech! Once approved by the states, these ten amendments became known as the Bill of Rights. Today there are twenty-seven amendments to the Constitution. [BTW: To change the Constitution, it takes an agreement from three-fourths of the states.]

⇨ **If two people disagree on the meaning of something in the Constitution, who gets the final say?** The Supreme Court. Now, it might begin in one of the lower courts, but if it's important enough, it will reach the biggest and baddest men and women in black!

OTHER QUICK BONUS FACTS!

⇨ Ben Franklin was the oldest person to sign the Constitution — he was eighty-one!

⇨ The youngest person to sign the Constitution was Jonathan Dayton from New Jersey, and he was twenty-six! Go Jon!

⇨ Like I said before, our Constitution is the oldest national document, but it's also the shortest!

⇨ Surprisingly, two of the Founding Fathers didn't sign the Constitution: Thomas Jefferson was chillin' in France, and John Adams was doing the same in England.

⇨ The original Constitution is housed in the National Archives Building in Washington DC.[4]

⇨ Nearly ten thousand amendments have been proposed, and only twenty-seven have passed into law![5] [So basically, that means the chances of changing the Constitution aren't very good.]

[For more information on the Constitution,
visit http://www.constitutionfacts.com.]

We Are Not a Democracy;

We Are a Democratic Republic!

[there's a difference]

A lot of Americans believe our government is a democracy, but that's not true. If America were a pure democracy, Al Gore would have become president in 2000. America is actually a democratic republic, which is "a limited government with enumerated powers (as specified in a Constitution) which is administered by persons elected by the people."[6] This basically means that the people vote through representatives [i.e., Congress for governing the country and electoral delegates for choosing a president], and these elected officials are supposed to represent the people [to the best of their ability] with their voice and vote. So the next time you're asked to discuss America's government [which is ALL the time, right?], make sure you know what we are — one democratic republic under God. [Well, at least that's what some say anyway!]

How a President Gets Elected: The Electoral College

[oh, and BTW: there is no actual college, like a university]

Electing a president every four years is a cumbersome task [think 2000], especially when one considers all the hoopla [think 2000] that begins almost two years prior to each presidential election year. The politics, the speculating, and the polling seem to start earlier and earlier with each election [think 2000]. But sadly, a lot of Americans aren't sure exactly how a president gets elected [um, think *2000*?] — in other words, few understand the inner workings of the Electoral College. We're definitely more *aware* of it since

2000, but there are still a good number of people who are a bit—how shall we say it?—clueless. Now, you don't really *have* to know all the inner workings, but there are a few essentials you need to understand. Here's a quick overview:

- In the Electoral College, each state has a certain number of electors* [this number is the same as the number of representatives a state has in Congress, from the House and Senate combined]. Compare, for example, Delaware and its three electoral votes with California, which has fifty-five electoral votes. This means candidates will more than likely spend *a great deal more time* in California than in Delaware [*if they go to Delaware at all—Delaware has been tracking closely with the Democratic line since 1992*].

- It should be noted that the total number of possible electors *never* changes [so the most votes a candidate could have if they won EVERY state would be 538]. However, every ten years when a census happens, if there are significant population shifts, one state might lose an electoral vote and another state might gain one. But the total number is always 538.

- For a candidate to win the presidential election, he or she must have 270 electoral votes. A state's electors usually will cast their votes toward the candidate who wins the

---

* *An elector is somebody who votes or is entitled to vote in an election.*

popular vote in their state, but that's not always been required. [*Today every state except Nebraska and Maine has a winner-take-all system!*]

🌀 Because each state has been given a different number of electoral votes, it's possible for a candidate to win the 270 votes needed to become president and *lose* the nation's overall popular vote. Again, think 2000!

Fun Facts About the Trends in the Electoral College!

⇨ What is it about Missouri? Whatever it is, since the 1904 presidential election [excluding 1956], Missouri has always sided with the winner, making the "Show Me State" a coveted backer in all presidential elections.

⇨ Indiana has almost always gone Republican.

⇨ On the other hand, The District of Columbia has almost always gone Democrat.

⇨ Southern States have traditionally gone Republican, while Oregon and Washington are usually pretty well locked up for the Democrats.

⇨ Ohio, Michigan, New Mexico, and, more recently, Florida are considered swing states, meaning they can go either way [*insert sexual joke here*].

Hail to the Chief:
What You Need to Know About
the Position of President

Have you ever met a president? My wife, Jessica, met President Clinton during his last year in office when she was the Wisconsin representative for Girls Nation. Her first encounter with him was surreal. Actually, she was somewhat amazed, really. Everything about him seemed polished and together: his handshake, his stature, the way he looked her directly in the eyes when she spoke to him. She said it was one of the most thrilling moments of her life.

Now, in many Christian circles, Bill Clinton is the equivalent to Pee-Wee Herman—and yes, he made some mistakes that gave David Letterman and Jay Leno a ton of late-night fodder—but I think it's rather sad that Christians have treated him with such disrespect. Though her meeting with Clinton lasted only a few seconds, Jessica says his entire demeanor was stellar. His past mistakes didn't devalue the position he held. I've seen President Bush speak on a couple of occasions. He's not the best speaker, not nearly as polished as Clinton, Reagan, or JFK, but his charm is in his ability to relate to just about anybody. Now, I certainly haven't agreed with every decision Bush has made during his term, but I still respect him, not because I think he's the greatest president to ever live but because I respect the position he holds. The position of president demands respect.

Contrary to somewhat popular belief, the executive branch is not simply the office of the president of the United States; it's much bigger than just the Oval Office. Most Americans think of it as simply "whatever happens in the White House," but when you vote for a president, you're voting for a man or woman who will appoint a lot of officials to many roles that ultimately will influence you. It's a more important decision than you may realize.

When I was a kid, I got terribly excited every time there was a presidential election; yeah, not only did I grow up a legalist, but I was also a nerd. Every four years while we stood in line at the voting booth, Dad gave me his lecture about the importance of what we were doing. "Other countries would give up a lot to be doing this right now, son," he'd say to me. "Don't take this freedom for granted." I kind of liked hearing Dad get passionate about stuff. I took those kinds of talks very seriously. It was like being a part of my very own Norman Rockwell painting, except without the root beer float, cute little puppy dog, and gray knickers. I believe one of the reasons I enjoyed presidential elections so much was because Dad loved taking me into the voting booth with him and letting me pull the levers. By the time I was eleven, I'd already voted for Ronald Reagan twice.

But since I was seven when I *first* "voted" for Reagan, I was rather oblivious to the power of his presidential position.

Little did I know back then that whoever becomes the president of the United States is often called the leader of the free world, mainly because the decisions he or she makes affect people all over the world. So in essence, when America chooses an "executive" leader, we are choosing someone who will certainly influence the world.

So what does the president do?

[here's the official job description according to the second article of the Constitution]

A Random Act of Trivia

QUESTION: Which president is best known for his words, "Speak softly and carry a big stick"?

  A. Teddy Roosevelt, just one of the presidents with a funny mustache
  B. Ronald Reagan, referring to his stance on the cold war
  C. John F. Kennedy, the only Catholic president to be elected
  D. Bill Clinton, talking about something Monica said to him

ANSWER: A. Teddy! You got it right, didn't you? Now turn this book right side up again.

⊞ Delivers information to Congress. [*This includes official stuff like security details, economic information, and great restaurant locations close to 1600 Pennsylvania Avenue.*]

⊞ Has the ability to convene both houses on "extraordinary occasions." [*The nerve of the president bothering Congress during the season finale of* Entourage!]

There are three official requirements [according to the Constitution]:

▶ Must be an American-born citizen. [Arnold can't be president. And neither can Celine Dion — so sad.]

▶ Must be thirty-five years old. [So more than likely you can't run yet.]

▶ Must have lived in the U.S. for the last fourteen years. [Aw, Madonna can't run — thank God!]

Now, might we suggest a few other requirements you should meet before you consider running for president?

▶ Be independently wealthy. You'll need a lot of money to make a serious run for the presidency.

▶ Be a believer in Crest Whitestrips! You never know when you'll have to smile big despite having been ripped to shreds by your competitor.

▶ Be sure to have a doting spouse, 2.7 kids, and be from the South! [The last president from the Northeast was John F. Kennedy — and that was a *long* time ago.]

▶ Be all that you can be. Some experience in the military might help the cause.

▶ Be good at Scrabble! [*You might learn how to spell* potato.]

■ Receives ambassadors from other countries. [*This can include dining with kings, taking chancellors to Graceland, or vomiting up bad sushi.*]

■ Acts as commander in chief of the armed forces. [*This means war.*]

■ Makes sure all laws are carried out. [*Working with Congress and state and local legislators to make sure our country remains safe.*]

It's got to be hard being president. The president certainly has other responsibilities beyond those listed in the Constitution. In fact, the president does many other things—actually important things, such as selecting Supreme Court justices when one dies or retires, choosing men and women for secretary positions that are in charge of all the important issues of our time, delivering the State of the Union

Thus far, being president in America has always required a certain willingness to be, umm, a little footloose and fancy *free* with the God-mentions. Especially when it's in the president's best interest to do so — like during the holidays, at the end of every major public appearance, and anytime he's on *Fox News*. From the saintly president [*cough, cough*] to the scandalous one [*cigars, anyone?*], every president must be able to bring everything back to the heavenly. So let's hail the power of political gain; let egos prostrate fall. 'Cause the bottom line is this: A big part of being political is learning the art of mixing a little church and state without letting the state know. Sound confusing? It is. But don't let it get you down; I'm here to guide you through proper "Godlitical" correctness in the twenty-first century.

Know the proper *God* holidays! You're free to talk about God during any of the following celebrations:

- ☒ **Fourth of July.** Fit in a God-mention right *after* the watermelon eating contest and *before* you go get yourself a fried Twinkie — *that's* the perfect time! And remember, Christians LOVE Twinkies!
- ☒ **Thanksgiving.** God usually likes his mention either *before* the gluttony or around kickoff.
- ☒ **Martin Luther King Jr. Day.** Anytime is the right time!
- ☒ **Presidents' Day.** God would prefer being mentioned right *after* you retell the story of Honest Abe and *before* Washington crossing the Delaware.
- ☒ **Saint Patrick's Day.** An exact time doesn't matter; just make sure it happens before the green beer gets flowing. And never mention God's name in the same sentence as a shamrock or leprechaun. *Oops.*
- ☒ Oh, and anytime there's a full moon!

BONUS RULE: Resist the temptation to mention God at Christmas, Easter, or the day after Thanksgiving.

Be ambiguous! Don't let anyone know *whose* God or "god" you're talking about. Smooth politicians never get caught with their faith down. To let their listeners know would be too potent a mixture of church and state, yet strangely God and country go together just fine.

Know your audience! For instance, if you're in the South, you can pretty much do a praise-and-worship dance on any street corner [except in Nashville because I live there]. If you're in the Northeast, only God with a small *g* is allowed. And if you're in Boston, please don't wear your "God is a Republican" T-shirt. I care about your well-being. And Boston's.

And lastly, if you're going to use God to gain political favor . . . Context and consistency are everything.

address every January [*and then getting spanked by the opposing party*], and acting as the nation's cheerleader, PR person, and visionary. And if you're president, you'd better be good at giving and listening to long speeches, leading and participating in long meetings, sitting through and acting like you're interested in long classical concerts, and dealing with lots of satire. Can you imagine knowing that *Saturday Night Live* is going to make fun of everything that comes out of your mouth?

But at least presidents normally get a month-long vacation in August. And besides, they *wanted* to become president, so it's their own darn fault.

Legislative Branch

[yippee, Congress!]

The second branch of our government is called the legislative branch! This branch works closely [*well, they're supposed to work closely*] with the executive branch in governing the national happenings of the United States. The legislative branch consists of two parts: the Senate and the House of Representatives. These two separate entities make up Congress! When it comes to the big C in Washington, it's often about lawmaking.

But Congress doesn't simply *make* laws; those who hold offices in the Senate and House have the responsibility of

Is the president just like all Americans? Well, maybe. But maybe not. We decided to take a tour of the president's house and Matthew's house and then compare the two. Here's what we found!

	White House	Matthew's house
To get to this house, you must . . .	Pass through security.	Pass by neighbor's pussy willow plant.
The first thing you'll notice:	Pretty shrubs and the nice green grass.	Dead houseplant outside the front door.
You'll be in awe of the . . .	Large columns, artwork, and decor.	Large red sofa and T.J.Maxx décor.
Number of rooms:	132.	If 6 closets are included, 11!
Number of bathrooms:	32.	2, and one is nicely decorated. And both come with fans!
Number of fireplaces:	28 for when the prez and his first lady want to get heated.	None, but good insulation!
Prior names:	President's Palace, the President's House, and the Executive Mansion.	The Love Shack, Groove Room, and Da Booty Digs.
Number of chefs:	5.	If you include the Food Network, 17.
Luxuries?	A tennis court, jogging track, swimming pool, movie theater, billiard room, and bowling lane.	The couches are very soft, warmth and coziness are always available, and NETFLIX!
In a resident's own words . . .	Harry Truman called the White House a "glamorous prison."	A former roommate called the Groove Room a "hot place to get my chill on."
Acreage?	18 acres.	Um, does the deck count?
Square footage?	55,000.	Just under 1,000.

managing and maintaining laws, too. In order for new laws to be made, existing laws to be changed, or old laws to be discarded, legislation [*the process of writing and passing laws*] must pass through both the House and the Senate *before* making it onto the president's desk. Members of Congress sit around all day and discuss laws, complain about laws, write changes to laws, make speeches about their proposed laws, attempt to gain support from other members for laws, and sometimes vote on laws.

Let's begin by talking about some basic details of the two sections of Congress.

The Senate

Members: 100. [2 per state; nope, the District of Columbia doesn't have representation.]

Term? 6 years, which sometimes seems like an eternity when you don't like your senator. [And they can run as many times as they want to.]

Powers: Though the House of Representatives has the power to impeach a president [in effect, act as prosecutor], it is the Senate that actually conducts impeachment trials [senators get to be the judge and jury]. The Senate also has the power to review, approve, or excuse a president's nominations for Supreme Court justices, ambassadors, public ministers, and all other United States officers. Senators also get to approve treaties that the president recommends or desires.

The House of Representatives

Members: 435. [Each state has a number that is dependent upon its population.]

Term? 2 years. [And no term limits!]

Powers: Yeah, so the reps make laws. And as already mentioned, they can also impeach the president.

Quick Look at How a Bill Gets Passed

▨ A concerned individual, group, or legislator has an idea and presents it to a representative or senator [depending on what this idea is — perhaps a war monument, increasing funds for cancer research, or a pay raise for, um, legislators — just letting it out of the bag can stir emotion].

▨ Then the representative or senator writes the idea into a bill. [Yeah, a bill is just an idea — you remember the *Schoolhouse Rock* song, right? You know, the one about the bill hanging out on Capitol Hill.]

▨ Then guess what happens? The bill gets introduced in either the House or the Senate! Deep stuff, huh?

▨ Each bill has a committee assigned to it: people from either the House or Senate. The committee reviews the bill and then reports on whether they are in favor or not in favor! Poor little bill then gets ridiculed a lot by mean men and women trying to keep it from becoming a law.

▨ At this point the committee can make changes to the bill. If changes are made, the bill then goes back to the originating chamber [House or Senate].

▨ Then the chamber where it originated votes on the bill. If it passes, it then gets sent to the other chamber for a vote. If it passes again, a conference committee made up of House and Senate members writes the final version of the bill!

▨ Of course, this is when the president either signs the bill into law or vetoes it and sends it back to Congress.

Actually, all the politics and drama that surround the making of laws is for our protection; the Founding Fathers called it a system of checks and balances. You remember that from tenth grade history, right?

What the Heck Does a Lobbyist Do?
Um, Well, We Asked One

Lobbyist Ryan Peebles, who is the director of government relations at the Information Technology Industry Council (ITI), says he LOVES moving and shaking Washington DC's elite. We communicated over e-mail about the basics of being a lobbyist.

MPT: Ryan, we hear a lot about lobbying in the news. Can you explain what a lobbyist does?

RYAN: Matthew, in simple terms, a lobbyist is a person or group of people seeking to influence or persuade politicians or people in public office. It's about believing in a cause and helping to educate congressional people about the issue you care about the most.

MPT: What types of causes can one lobby for or against?

RYAN: The possibilities are limitless when it comes to causes or issues. In my experience, politics touches everybody in some way, form, or fashion, which is the reason there are lobbyists representing every issue that faces Congress. From business to the environment to entertainment, there are lobbyists for everything.

MPT: What kinds of accountability do lobbyists have?

RYAN: Federal lobbyists register with the clerk of the House and the secretary of the Senate. We are required to abide by the rules of The Lobbying Disclosure Act of 1995 (LDA), and that includes disclosing to our clients and/or our organizations what we represent and the issues we are working on. We are also required to file any financial expenditures when entertaining members of Congress, administration officials, or their staffs.

MPT: What would you say to people who believe lobbying is manipulative?

RYAN: The word *manipulate* suggests that we are influencing unfairly. I don't see it that way. We simply persuade the member of Congress why an issue is important to his or her district, state, or the country. The member then will make the best decision based on a number of factors — financial, political, social, and so forth.

MPT: Why are lobbyists an important part of the political process?

RYAN: I think we play a vital role in the process. People need to understand that we are educators. In most instances, lobbyists are experts in their respective fields and offer valuable information so that a member of Congress can make the best possible decisions for his or her constituents. If I were a member of Congress, I would want to be thoroughly educated on all sides of the issue before casting a vote on the House or Senate floor.

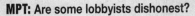

MPT: Are some lobbyists dishonest?

RYAN: It's sad to say that some are, but I don't think lobbyists are any more dishonest than people in any other profession as a whole. When lobbyists screw up, it is probably more publicized than in most professions because America is intrigued by scandals that originate in and around government.

MPT: What's the best and worst thing about being a lobbyist?

RYAN: If you asked one hundred lobbyists the same question, I'm sure you would get one hundred different answers, but let me give it a shot. The best: I have enjoyed the relationships I have built with the members of Congress and their staffs. I truly have become a more complete individual and have learned so much from the people I have met and worked with in Washington. And I love being part of the process. It is gratifying to watch a piece of legislation that you worked so hard on go through the House and the Senate and eventually be signed into a law that benefits businesses, jobs, the economy, families, and America. The worst: The same process I just described can be your greatest disappointment. It can be frustrating when your piece of legislation gets compromised and/or killed and you have to go back to the drawing board. You have to be patient with the process.

The Judicial Branch —
Here Comes the Judge
[actually, nine of them]

The judicial branch of the United States government is the branch of government we most enjoy watching [on shows like *The People's Court*] and least want to actually be a part of [have you ever had to do jury duty? Yikes! It's even more boring than learning about politics]. Our government certainly wouldn't function as well without the judicial branch. In the framework of the Constitution, the legislative branch makes the laws, the executive branch enforces the laws, and the judicial branch interprets and applies the laws. In real-life terms, what this means is that the judicial branch is in charge of resolving disputes — between two citizens, between citizens and the government, or between any parties that disagree on what the law actually means. Since, as I said before, arguments, debates, and disagreements are basically foundational to our political system [that's pretty much what "balance of power" means], the judicial branch is pretty important.

Incidentally, the way the judicial branch works is also based on argument. The judicial branch functions by an adversarial method, which means that it resolves disputes by bringing the two parties who disagree together in front of a third, neutral party and basically letting them duke it out. [Not literally, of course—they have lawyers duke it out for them. Unless, of course, they're on *Judge Judy*, in which case they might get into a physical fight, although it will probably be outside the courtroom.]

Here are some facts about the organization of the judicial branch:

- The Supreme Court is the ultimate court of appeal in the judicial branch. That means it's the most important: What the Supreme Court says goes. [*You don't piss off these men and women!*]
- Under the Supreme Court, there are thirteen U.S. Courts of Appeals and thirteen U.S. Courts of Appeals for the Armed Forces. These are the first courts you can go to if you don't agree with a decision made in a lower court.
- Under the courts of appeals are the ninety-four district courts. Usually when you go to court for the first time, this will be the court you go to—if it's a federal case.
- Most cases are tried in state courts. The ninety-four federal district courts hear only original cases that can't be tried in a state court—cases that involve the U.S. government, the Constitution, Congress or treaties, and disagreements between states or between our government and foreign governments, as well as disagreements involving a citizen of another country.

And some facts about the Supreme Court:

- Supreme Court justices, like all federal judges, are appointed for life. It was set up this way to help the balance of powers in the government [so the president can't just get rid of all the judges he doesn't like]. However, judges can be impeached if they're found to have behaved in an unethical manner.
- Ethical behavior for federal judges was established by the Code of Conduct for United States Judges adopted by the Judicial Conference of the United States.
- There are about five thousand appeals to the Supreme Court each year. Of those, the Court hears about one hundred.
- The Supreme Court begins on the first Monday in October and works until the business of that term is concluded—usually late June or July.

And finally, some facts about juries and trials:

- Both civil and criminal defendants are guaranteed the right to a trial by jury. They can, however, choose to waive that right [but if my lawyer told me to waive it, I think I'd find a new lawyer].
- There are two types of juries: petit juries and grand juries.
- Petit juries are the twelve-person juries you're familiar with

from the movies *Twelve Angry Men* and *Runaway Jury*. They weigh evidence and decide whether or not a defendant is guilty [in a criminal case] or liable [in a civil case].

Grand juries don't have a set number of members; they can have as many as twenty-three people [which would mean the movie would have been titled *Twenty-Three Angry Men*, and it would have been a lot angrier]. They don't oversee an actual trial; instead, they look at the evidence and decide whether or not there's sufficient reason to issue a formal indictment against a suspect in a criminal case. Some states require that a grand jury look at the evidence and make the decision; other states allow

Famous Campaign Slogans

[with jokes]

⇨ "No child left behind." George W. Bush [*Let's do ourselves a favor and believe this one could still happen!*]

⇨ "A kinder, gentler America." George H. W. Bush [*Ha ha ha ha ha!*]

⇨ "Nothing to fear but fear itself." Franklin D. Roosevelt [*Wait a minute! This one's in the Bible, right?*]

⇨ "Ask not what your country can do for you." John F. Kennedy [*Katrina victims learned that one the hard way!*]

⇨ "It's the economy, stupid." Bill Clinton [*With Bill, you can pretty much replace any word for the word* economy! *OR for the word* stupid.]

⇨ "Speak softly and carry a big stick." Teddy Roosevelt [*Um, I won't go there.*]

⇨ "Are you better off than you were four years ago?" Ronald Reagan [*This is figuratively, right?*]

⇨ "A chicken in every pot." Herbert Hoover [*Hee hee. He said "pot."*]

the prosecuting lawyer to file the indictment himself.

◎ In a civil case, the prosecutor must show a "preponderance of evidence" or "clear and convincing evidence" that the defendant is liable. Criminal cases must prove "beyond a reasonable doubt" that the defendant is guilty.[7]

Final Thought
[of section 1]

Having three separate branches of government is one of the greatest advantages of the United States political system. Like a stool with three legs, the three branches help balance the complicated business of politics much better and more solidly than two legs could. The old saying goes that "two's company and three's a crowd," but in the case of politics, a crowd can be a good thing. [For one thing, you can't really have a democracy without a crowd, and you certainly can't have a vote without at least three people since you need to break the tie, but that's not exactly what I'm getting at here.]

I said earlier that politics always involve an argument of some kind, and if you look at our political history and our political system today, it's obvious that no one is better than politicians at getting into disagreements and fights. When two people argue, it's difficult to ever come to a conclusion [as you know if you're married]—the two parties can keep going back and forth about their opposing opinions till doomsday. Three people, however, are more likely to be able to come to a conclusion because two of them can gang up on the other. We see that all the time in modern politics: If the Republicans have control of both the presidency and the House, they like to gang up on the Democrats in the Senate.

But that's where the beauty of our political system comes in. In order for a bill to become law, it has to be passed by both the House and the Senate—which makes it a lot harder for two groups to gang up on another. Even if the House and Senate both agree, the president can veto something he doesn't like [although he gets looked down on if he uses that power a lot]. And finally, once something has passed into law, the Supreme Court still has the power to interpret and apply the law as it sees fit. So although our three branches tend to make the political process a lot more complicated, they also make it a lot safer and more stable; it's hard for any one group or faction to do too much damage.

Dang! Did you like all that social studies? Well, it only gets better! It's time for GOD to enter the picture. The next section is on faith and politics.

Politics, the Bible, and Christianity

[God's politics . . . well, not really, but at least some points of view on his politics]

> The United States is in no sense founded upon the Christian doctrine.
>
> — George Washington

Politics gets mentioned a lot in churches across America. It's like a fifth spiritual law, really. You know, first, God loves you. And second, you are sinful. If you can handle that last one, you should know this, too: Only Jesus can save you from sin. And finally, if you decide to accept him as your Savior — *ding ding ding* — you win a bonus law: During years when there is a presidential election, follow the Republican Party, my newly reborn child! [*That's supposed to be God talking. But not really.*]

[Okay, so there are some churches that say the same thing about the Democratic Party. But for some reason, it seems to be mostly the Republican Party. No one really knows exactly why that is, but the Republicans sure like it.]

Why do we Christians get so excited about politics? Whatever the reason, we certainly go all out the moment God reveals his political leanings in an election year. And thankfully, he makes it easy for us; there's no secret code that we have to figure out, no long book that we have to read, and God apparently doesn't even think we're smart enough for long sentences. God just calls his printer in Dallas and asks him to create a bunch of bumper stickers with his political support written in clear, easy-to-read language. But the really strange thing is that God *also* has a printer in Connecticut. *Go figure.* And of course, the two messages contradict.

GOD VOTES REPUBLICAN!

GOD VOTES DEMOCRAT!

As I've stated on a couple of other occasions within this book, the church I grew up in combined politics and the Bible like one was a martini and the other a green olive. Of course, I'm not going to tell you which was the martini and which was the olive; that might get me into trouble. [Not that the thought of getting into a little trouble has stopped me before.]

But as I was saying, my old pastor enjoyed mixing politics with his sermons. He used the Bible to prove just about everything. Sometimes he was rather creative in dappling his messages with conservative jargon. Like the time he preached about Nehemiah building the wall. He stopped right in the middle of a thought and said, "Nehemiah wasn't afraid of doing the impossible, so let's just take a moment and thank God that we have a man in the White House who *isn't* afraid of a little hard work." He was referring to Ronald Reagan and his fight against the Democrats for the Star Wars program. Now, a little politics in church might seem harmless, but over time, many in my church became desensitized to hearing politics proclaimed from the pulpit. [They also got conditioned into believing that my pastor's political leanings were 100 percent correct.]

But it's not only conservative politics that get mixed with church; liberal politics show up as well. Usually this begins quietly through pastoral musings about the love of Jesus but quickly bounces away from the simple gospel message and ends with a rather unfortunate mix-up between Jesus' love being able to reach every ugly nook and cranny of our lives [which is true] and it showing up in the form of political rallies, feminism, and apathy [which are all unproven or simply an altered version of Jesus' love].

Recently, the church has become blatant in its pursuit of sermonizing politics, which often leads to confusion as to how we can emulate Jesus within our culture without selling out to a political party, sounding like a fanatic, or seeming wishy-washy in our spirituality. These feelings can often overwhelm us so much that we end up becoming bitter toward the entire political process.

But don't do that, at least not just yet. [*I will let you know when it's time to become bitter; you and I can have a party! Ooh, the Bitter Party!*] Despite it not being written by the likes of Ann Coulter or Al Franken [*thank God*], the Bible does indeed

Moses	Bush
Met wife while attending to his sheep.	Met wife while attending to his cattle.
Received Ten Commandments on a mountain.	Really enjoys hiking in the mountains.
Motto: "I carry a staff; so, God is with me."	Motto: "God is on my staff; he sits next to Condoleezza."
Turned the Nile River into blood for several days!	Allowed New Orleans to remain a lake for several days!
Led people out of Egypt.	Led people into Iraq.
Heard God speak from a bush.	Was born a Bush!

discuss politics rather extensively. Now, the Bible's not a political commentary written in narrative, like *Gulliver's Travels* or *Animal Farm*; nor is it a political memoir like Bill Clinton's *My Life*. But it's still filled with information that is useful on this journey.

And some of it is not useful at all. Well, at least not to your current political view. But you might find it helpful in other areas of your life.

So, um, let's make like the U.S. Army and begin the *biblical* shock and awe!

 Okay, that was dumb; let's just dive in.

An Introduction of Biblical Proportion
Themes in the Bible That Are Related to Politics

Two ideas in the Bible are central to the concept of all political activities: relationships and power. [*And, of course, campaign slogans: We Shall Overcome! Thou Shalt Not Commit Adultery! And even, Deliver Us from Evil! And, of course, NO CHILD LEFT BEHIND! Which I hear is a new book being written by Tim LaHaye.*]

As I've mentioned before, politics are always relational; that's because they deal with the interaction of individuals and societies. You see, people much smarter than me [*and more experienced at politicking*] have described politics as a social contract [*John Locke said that one*], as a decision-making process, and as a means of conflict resolution [*another way of resolving conflicts is to beat up anyone who disagrees with you, but that's not a very nice thing for people in the Bible to be doing — but sometimes they did it anyway*]. So politics are essentially interaction, and anytime people come together as a group, politics come into play.

Okay, let's get a little philosophical for a moment. Power is the dark side of politics. Whether it's the struggle among different players to gain power or the top-down exercise of rightful authority, politics are about gaining and giving, winning and losing. Someone comes out on top — and someone doesn't. Ideally the interaction will conclude in a way that is beneficial to both parties, but in every political outcome, there are benefits and losses, usually for both sides. That's why politics have been explained as a social contract: Both sides are willing to give something up for a greater good — the good of society or benefits for individuals that outweigh the sacrifices. Or at least that's the way it's supposed to be. Unfortunately it doesn't always work like that.

Truth to Know

Be a good citizen. All governments are under God. Insofar as there is peace and order, it's God's order. So live responsibly as a citizen. If you're irresponsible to the state, then you're irresponsible with God, and God will hold you responsible. Duly constituted authorities are only a threat if you're trying to get by with something. Decent citizens should have nothing to fear.

Do you want to be on good terms with the government? Be a responsible citizen and you'll get on just fine, the government working to your advantage. But if you're breaking the rules right and left, watch out. The police aren't there just to be admired in their uniforms. God also has an interest in keeping order, and he uses them to do it. That's why you must live responsibly — not just to avoid punishment but also because it's the right way to live.

That's also why you pay taxes — so that an orderly way of life can be maintained. Fulfill your obligations as a citizen. Pay your taxes, pay your bills, respect your leaders.

(Romans 13:1-7)

Wanna Lean a Little More to the Left?

[three books you might consider adding to your personal library]

- ◆ *God's Politics* by Jim Wallis — "Compelling!"
- ◆ *Red and Blue God, Black and Blue Church* by Becky Garrison — "Funny! Thoughtful! Um, controversial!"
- ◆ *The Politics of Jesus* by John Howard Yoder — "Poignant words about Jesus' lasting effect on our society."

Wanna Lean a Little More to the Right?

[two books you might consider adding to your personal library]

- ☆ *Godless* by Ann Coulter — "Entertaining! And to the point!"
- ☆ *The Holy Vote* by Ray Suarez — "Good research. Interesting detail!"

Three Perspectives on Politics and the Bible

[can we get deep for a moment?]

Politics from the Beginning ...

Now, you know this, but it's worth repeating. The topics of relationships and power are addressed repeatedly in the Bible from the very beginning of the first book.

Consider the life and times of Adam. Can you imagine being all alone among God's creation? Neither could God, I suppose; he deemed it not good for Adam to be alone. He was in need of relationship to become complete. You know the story. It's perhaps the weirdest series of events possible: God put Adam to sleep, took out one of his ribs, and out of somewhere — *we're not sure we want to know where* — popped woman. And it's through Eve that relationship was provided.

Enter politics. *Some might say dirty politics.*

As soon as sin entered the picture, relationships became laced with conflict. Right at the beginning of God's narrative, we see struggle and compromise, relationship and power. Cain and Abel introduced the first sibling rivalry, and politics came into play with a vengeance — literally. Cain's jealousy was politically motivated: He was frustrated with the fact that his brother was higher up on the divine political ladder, evidenced by the fact that Cain's sacrifice wasn't accepted by God and Abel's sacrifice was. On a mythical level, the story of Cain and

✪ ✪ ✪ ✪ ✪ ✪ ✪ ✪ ✪ ✪ ✪ ✪ ✪ ✪ ✪ ✪ ✪

This is L. C. Baker again. I just wanted to clarify this because I *know* somebody's going to read this and say, "Wait a minute! Did he just compare the Bible to mythology? That means he doesn't believe the Bible! Heretic! Stone him!" And while I have to admit that I might occasionally have the urge to stone Matthew Paul Turner [or at least ignore his phone calls], he is my friend as well as my coauthor. So let me reassure you on behalf of the writers and editors of this book: We do believe the Bible. In fact, most of us believe that much of the Bible is literally and historically true. However, it's legitimate to read history — *especially* history that someone [like God] thought was worth preserving in an ancient Scripture like the Bible — from a mythical as well as a historical perspective. J. R. R. Tolkien explained this perspective well when he described the Bible as a true myth.[1] Looking at the Bible from this perspective doesn't mean that you can't believe it happened historically; it just means you can also look at the story on a deeper level to learn what it can teach you from a literary, cultural, and mythical perspective. And if that's a little deep for a book on politics, well, sorry. We writers get into this kind of thing; sometimes we just can't help ourselves.

✪ ✪ ✪ ✪ ✪ ✪ ✪ ✪ ✪ ✪ ✪ ✪ ✪ ✪ ✪ ✪ ✪ ✪

Abel has plenty of political and social undertones: It indicates a preference for the wandering herder over the stable farmer, a bias against settled civilization, a prejudice against cities.[2]

This prejudice shows itself in other stories throughout Genesis: the Flood, the tower of Babel, Sodom and Gomorrah. All of them, on a symbolic level, are expressions of the danger of civilization, of settled towns, of organized government: the danger of the *polis*, of the city.

The danger, in other words, of politics. *Da da da dum!*

The First Perspective: Withdrawal
The stories in Genesis answer this danger of politics in several ways. But probably the most common response is retreat from the city. Yes, many of the stories in Genesis present God's people as ones who are supposed to run for their little lives. Consider the following:

- Noah is told to flee the wrath to come (see 6–8).
- Abram is called by God to leave his country and his people (see 13–14).
- Lot is warned to leave the evil city before it's destroyed (see 19).

It's a drastic response, but it's one we definitely see in Scripture: Sometimes when things get really bad, the only thing to do is to get out of town. One of the responses of godly people in the Bible to the evils of politics is withdrawal and isolation.

In today's world, withdrawal and isolation are options that often seem tempting. [*And actually, between you and me, I wish some Christians would take those options. Yes, I know that was mean; I'm sorry. (Sort of.)*] And many Christians do take this route. There are extreme exam-  ples, like Amish towns [*beep, beep: horse and buggy coming through*], and there are less extreme examples, like families who homeschool their children [*and make them enter the National Spelling Bee and National Geography contest*] and those who move to  small-town America [*and pursue farming despite having never grazed anything in their lives except the racks at Macy's*]. Of course, there are also those Christians who live in holes in the ground in places like West Virginia and Wyoming, stockpiling water and canned goods and waiting for utter destruction to hit.

Throughout history, this instinct to retreat, this desire to withdraw from the evil in the world, has been a refuge for many. People who adhere to this type of thinking often wonder, *What else can one do in the face of so much evil?* And I certainly sometimes understand this sentiment. But does this type of thinking make sense? Are there other options? Unable to influence the culture, are we left with no choice but to remove ourselves from it as quickly as possible? [*I'll get to this answer soon enough.*]

L. C. Baker here with a confession. I'm really glad Matthew brought this topic up. I have to admit there are moments when the idea of retreating from the world sounds really attractive to me. It's not necessarily that the world is so evil; it's just that our way of life in America sometimes seems so materialistic, consumeristic, individualistic, and, well, all those other -istics, that I'm not sure I want to be a part of it anymore. I can understand the mentality of people who decide to just get away from it all, no matter how they choose to do it. For example, for much of the time we've been working on this book, I've been house-sitting on a farm. There's something really fun, something earthy and real and honest, about gathering eggs every morning and then cooking those very eggs for breakfast. Until, of course, the rooster attacks you [*I swear this really did happen to me*], flies at your foot [*so he's a bantam rooster; he's really small*], and scratches your leg. Okay, maybe it's back to the grocery store for now. Retreating from the world can be a lot harder than it looks from the outside. But that doesn't mean it can't be a good idea.

 [sometimes our theology can affect our politics]

One approach to this solution of withdrawal from the world has gained popularity in recent times through the best-selling novel series *Left Behind*. [*Let's all say, "Left Behind."*] As some sixty million people have read, these books present vivid pictures of the end of the world as seen through a premillennial dispensationalist eschatology.*

Now, I know what you're probably thinking: *Um, Matthew, so how does* Left Behind *affect a person's politics? And what the heck is a premillennial dispensationalist eschatology?* Well, if that's what you're thinking, then you are in luck because I'm going to explain that right now. *Well, maybe not the premillennial dispensationalist eschatology part, because I'm not entirely sure what it is either.* However, in the *Left Behind* version of the end times, all Christians on earth are raptured [*taken away, leaving articles of clothes everywhere — it's really quite messy*] up to heaven [*yeah, according to* Left Behind, *we'll be entering heaven buck naked*] and after they're gone, the rest of the world is plunged into utter chaos and confusion. And then the world is united under the Antichrist in a lead-up to the final battle between Satan and God [*when all hell breaks loose*]. Although not all interpretations of biblical prophecy are as literal as this version, the fact remains: Your expectation of the end of the world is bound to influence your politics.

---

* *This is the focus of religious doctrine concerning the destiny of the human soul as it relates to death, judgment, heaven, and hell.*

If you live life by a belief that ultimately the world is going to hell in a hand basket and the best you can hope to do is hold off the storm a little longer, then for you, politics is a big ole waste of time. I mean, from that perspective, it might actually be better for the world to get worse instead of better because, like a blister that has to pop before it can heal, everything will have to get as bad as it can possibly be before Jesus will come to make everything right. According to that philosophy, it's better to withdraw from politics and let the world go on making a mess of things. Once things get bad enough, God will come and fix it.

>>[**Disclaimer:** Please know that not all views expressed in this book are the views of Matthew Paul Turner, L. C. Baker, or TH1NK Books. We're simply trying to give you a broad – eh, dramatic – picture of how some Christians interpret Scripture and how those views **affect their politics.**]<<

But come on, if withdrawal is the only answer to the problems of politics, then there's no reason for this book to exist. Fortunately, the Bible does offer other alternatives to the problems of civilization than to become a separatist.

The Second Perspective: Influence

The second response to politics that is offered in the Bible is the option of influence. Yes, I know what you're thinking: *Of course, we're all supposed to influence others through our faith,*

The Editors Present: Best Old Testament Political Scandals [and when we say best, we mean most notable!]

Winner of . . .	Who and what?	Why on the list?	What Clinton might say
Best scandal involving a wife	Abraham telling leaders of a city that Sarah [his wife] was his sister.	Because the king of the city ended up taking Sarah to be his wife.	"I never had sexual relations with my sister."
Best scandal involving the color red	Rahab helping save Israelite spies from Jericho destruction.	Because Rahab was a prostitute.	"A prostitute, huh?"
Best scandal involving a prophet	Elijah predicts that King Ahab and Queen Jezebel will die and their bodies will be eaten by dogs.	Because according to Scripture, it happened.	"I just thank the good Lord that Elijah wasn't around during my presidency. Dog bites suck."
Best scandal involving nudity	David's affair with Bathsheba.	He ended up having her husband killed in battle.	"I did not have sexual relations with that Bathsheba."
Best scandal involving lions	King Darius throwing Daniel in the lions' den.	The lions didn't kill Daniel.	"I like this story. Those conservative right-winged lions didn't eat me, either. Well, they nibbled, but that's it."
Best scandal involving foreskin	David's gift of two hundred Philistine foreskins to Saul.	The fact that foreskins were a gift.	"Hmm, I do know a few uncircumcised Republicans. But don't ask me how."

right? Well, yes. But right now we're talking about politics. And you'll probably agree that using our faith to influence doesn't always take a political form—we're not all lobbyists, activists, or politicians. However, there are examples in the Bible of godly people whose response to evil politics took exactly those forms—or at least the ancient versions of them. Their response to politics was to *get involved*, sometimes on the highest levels.

This response is most obvious in the story of Joseph, but you can also see it in the stories of Esther and Daniel. These were men and women of God who chose to influence, rather than escape from, the bad politics in the city. Joseph found himself, through no choice of his own, forced to live in a foreign country. He ended up there pretty much because of the worst kind of dirty politics: family politics. His brothers were jealous of him as the favorite son, and they thought their father might like *them* better if they got rid of *him*. However, God blessed Joseph everywhere he went, and he ended up being influential no matter where he was—whether in a centurion's household, in prison, or in the pharaoh's palace. Eventually, he gained so much influence that he was able to change the politics and policies of the entire nation, ensuring happiness, health, and wealth for both himself and his reunited family. [*But don't read this happy ending as an argument for the health-and-wealth gospel; just because God did it for Joseph doesn't necessarily mean he'll do it for you! I mean, just look at my bank account.*]

Esther, too, was forced into a position of importance and influence by situations beyond her control [*she won a beauty contest—yay—which apparently included not only a swimsuit competition but also a sex competition—yikes*], but she used that influence to change the laws of the nation and the heart of the king. And Daniel, similarly, got his influence because he was wise. These stories don't necessarily say that politics are a good thing, but they do show that good people can use politics to serve God and help others.

As far as eschatology goes [*remember, that's what a person believes about the end of the world*], Christians who believe it's important to influence politics might have different opinions, but they usually have a less literal interpretation of end-times prophecies. They might believe that many of the end-times prophecies have actually already happened. Or they might believe that these prophecies will be fulfilled in the future but that it's our responsibility as Christians to work together with God to help set the stage for Jesus' return. Either way, they believe it's important for Christians to work to change politics and to make a difference in the world.

God's Spirit is on me;
    he's chosen me to preach the
        Message of good news to the
        poor,
Sent me to announce pardon to
    prisoners and
        recovery of sight to the blind,
To set the burdened and battered free,
    to announce, "This is God's year
        to act!"
(Luke 4:18-19)

One type of politics that deserves mention here is a method of influencing the world that's popular in oppressed communities: the way of resistance. Resistance finds its most obvious expression in liberation theology, which uses two biblical stories as the prime examples for us to follow: the story of the Exodus and the story of the Cross. Although there are several aspects of liberation theology that are not necessarily in line with orthodox Christianity—especially its understanding of the Incarnation and the Cross—it's a very influential movement in the interaction of theology and politics.

Liberation theology is a theology of the oppressed. It sees the world as divided into oppressed and oppressor, and it insists that God is always on the side of the oppressed. God is not only for the poor, but he is revealed in the poor. Therefore, the call of the church is toward liberation, toward freedom, and toward helping the poor and oppressed. Sin occurs when man is inhumane toward other men, and salvation is defined in secular, physical, and political terms. In liberation theology, to be saved means to be freed from slavery and bondage. So a big part of the church's job is political. The task of the church is to free the prisoners and the oppressed. In this theology, God can be seen or known only through the faces of the poor, and our knowledge of God comes through action rather than study or knowledge.[3]

Although liberation theology has been condemned as unorthodox, it has also contributed a lot to the Christian understanding of politics. It calls for resistance on the part of the church to anything that allows a continuation of an unjust status quo. Unlike mere influence, which makes use of existing political structures, resistance seeks to overturn unjust structures and create a new structure, one that isn't inherently oppressive.

This choice to get directly involved in and influence politics—whether subtly or overtly—seems to have been a rare occurrence in the Bible, usually one that individuals were forced into by circumstances beyond their control. However, it has frequently been the most attractive option for modern Christians.

The desire to change culture, to influence politics, to bring society more into line with God's intentions has been the dream of the church's political involvement in modern times. Many Christians want to transform America into a modern

"Tell us: Is it lawful to pay taxes to Caesar or not?"

He knew they were laying for him and said, "Show me a coin. Now, this engraving, who does it look like and what does it say?"

"Caesar," they said.

Jesus said, "Then give Caesar what is his and give God what is his." (Luke 20:22-25)

theocracy, a place where biblical values and Christian ethics dominate every aspect of law and culture. We picture a place where abortions happen only in history books, where marriage is defined in biblical terms by a constitutional amendment, and where poverty and inequality are only memories. Today there are movements by people on both sides of the political spectrum whose visions come from the same seed: the desire to build a more Christian government. It is the dream of many modern Christians to be like Esther and Daniel, to have a place of leadership and prominence and to change society for the better.

Is this a realistic dream? Is it in line with biblical values? One thing to consider is that it is based on situations that were relatively rare in the Bible. Of course, that doesn't mean that it's wrong or unattainable. However, there is a third option that happens more often in Scripture.

The Third Perspective: A Combo of One and Two? Thy Kingdom Come?

The third way of Christian politics as pictured in the Bible is a combination of withdrawal and influence: the way of a new kingdom. This is the relationship between godly people and politics that occurs the most in Scripture. From Moses and the Exodus to Jesus' talk of the kingdom, we see the dream of establishing a new society, creating a new way of living, building a new kingdom.

Some people call this kingdom living!

In the Old Testament, this new kingdom was firmly grounded in the social and political realm. It consisted of a group of people who were set free by the Exodus to become a new nation, a nation that was governed by God. They got their laws directly from God himself—and I'm not just talking about the Ten Commandments. There were laws that covered pretty much every detail of their lives, from fashion [*using two types of fabric in the same piece of clothing was forbidden, which means that those fancy two-tone leather shoes were out!*] to hairstyles [*remember Sampson's infamous haircut?*] to bodily functions [*yeah, um . . . you can look it up*]. Anyway, the Old Testament kingdom of Israel really was a theocracy in the truest sense—it was a nation that was governed by God. The nation of Israel was meant to show the world exactly what politics *ought* to be.

[*Sounds heavenly, right? Um, maybe not.*]

 In modern times, this idea of a theocracy, and the desire to recreate it, has often been the motivation of Christian political action. The focus of the Religious Right on homosexuality and abortion and the focus of the Christian Left on poverty and pacifism are both motivated by this desire to build God's kingdom on a political scale. The Religious Right wants to see the Ten Commandments, the moral handbook of the Old Testament theocracy, become the legislative standard in America. The Christian Left wants to see the Old Testament practices of caring for the poor and oppressed become central to the American way of life.

But should we really take ancient Israel as the best example for the modern American political system? In the Old Testament, the relationship between politics and theology was simple: Beliefs—and God's commands—should influence and even dictate government. A righteous man was marked by his attention to the poor and by his obedience to God's laws, and a good king was one who remembered, followed, and enacted God's laws. Things were straightforward because Israel was more than just a political entity—it was also a group of people living in a covenantal relationship with God.

In Jesus' day, the Old Testament paradigm of the direct relationship between God's kingdom and the earthly, political kingdom was widely believed and mostly unchallenged. That is why Jesus' talk of a kingdom that was *literally* "not of this world" (John 18:36, NIV) was so puzzling to his followers. His insistence that the kingdom was "already among you" (Luke 17:21) and "within you" (Matthew 3:11) was utterly foreign to their ideas of a political kingdom.

Jesus' words contradicted every hope his disciples had for the establishment of a real-world divine government. When his followers tried to make him king, he ran away and hid from them. And when his enemies accused him before the established government, the Roman Empire, of rebelling against the throne, he neither admitted nor denied it, but he also didn't resist their punishment. He went quietly to his death — the death of a political radical, the death of a revolutionary.

After that, of course, Jesus' disciples figured out what's clear to us today: When he said his kingdom was not of this world, he meant it. Our job as Christians is not to establish a theocracy in America. The Old Testament example of Israel actually has a lot more in common with the modern church than with the modern political system. The kingdom of God today is seen not in political systems but in the living community of people who love and follow God. The kingdom is about people living a new way of life and being an example to the world.

But is it possible that we're missing something in this picture? Yes, his kingdom is not of this world. But history seems to indicate that the kingdom of Christ did have a lot more impact on the kingdoms of this world than we generally think about. From the time of the Cross and onward, the relationship between Christianity and politics has been at best shaky and at worst hostile. Consider this:

- The very phrase "Jesus is Lord" was probably first used as a deliberate political assertion: It's a takeoff [and a rejection] of the Roman cry of loyalty, "Caesar is Lord." It was no accident that Christianity had no sooner begun to establish itself and spread than it fell under persecution — not by other religions, but by the government.
- The Roman Empire was notoriously tolerant of the various religions and beliefs it gathered under its political system — those tolerant policies were crucial to its success. Every religion, including monotheistic ones like Judaism, was willingly accepted into the polytheism of the Romans. But Christianity quickly became a bloody exception to those policies as Christians were shortly made the good sport of being thrown to the lions. Why? The only

logical explanation is that Christians were, in the minds of the emperors, becoming a threat in the same way that other victims of the gladiatorial ring were a threat: not a religious threat or a social one but a threat to the political system—a threat to the power of the emperor.

Now, since then, Christianity has walked a fine line between obedience and opposition. Both the apostle Peter and the apostle Paul spoke about how interaction with the government should be. Peter urged readers of his letters to "honor the king" (1 Peter 2:17), but when instructed by the government to stop teaching in Jesus' name, he replied, "We must obey God rather than men!" (Acts 5:29, NIV). In a similar manner, Paul encouraged others to live "quiet lives" (1 Timothy 2:2, NIV), and yet *he himself spent the majority of his adult life in prison for his refusal to obey the king's orders to stop preaching.*

More than anything, it is this priority of loyalties that exemplifies the political nature of being a Christian. As far as it's possible, we are urged to "live at peace with everyone" (Romans 12:18, NIV)—but there might come a point when it is no longer possible, and if that moment comes, then we have to know where our loyalties lie. As Christians, "our citizenship is in heaven" (Philippians 3:20, NIV), which means that our loyalty is first to God, not to the government of the country where we happen to live.

Meet Some of Christianity's Most Politically Active Conservative Individuals

Most everyone knows the names of the individuals in the following chart. [*Well, you may not know one of them — I'll let you guess which one.*] If you don't, you should; these seven individuals are known for making a case for God and country in the public square. Of course, sometimes they have a hard time doing that without offending large populations of people. But as is the case with most Christian conservatives, there's always a back-story. And the editors of *What You Didn't Learn from Your Parents About Politics* have the scoop. [*Well, as is the case with most of what the editors write, they sort of have the scoop.*]

	Pat Robertson	Ann Coulter	Ralph Reed
Political role	TV host.	Right-wing commentator.	Conservative spin doctor.
On any given day, he or she is . . .	Prophesying on national TV.	Showing off her legs on national television.	Searching for jobs on Monster.com.
One word often associated with him or her	Huh?	*Godless.*	Youthful.
In his or her perfect world . . .	Church and state would sleep together. And by golly, they would like it.	Matt Lauer would be served as an hors d'oeuvre at her next book party.	He'd be lieutenant governor of Georgia!
If running for president, his or her campaign slogan might be . . .	Destruction is coming to America in 2012!	America is great because America knows me. If America ceases to know me, then catch me on MSNBC — *usually on Tuesdays!*	Who is Ralph Reed?
On his or her iPod you'd find . . .	ABBA [*He thought it was a record by God.*]	Ann Coulter's *Godless.*	Madonna.
Known for	*The 700 Club.*	Being funny and conservative.	Being the first executive director of the Christian Coalition.
Still relevant?	The millions of Christians who support him think so!	Yep. Her edgy right talk has made her a conservative icon.	He hopes so.

	Jerry Falwell	Kenneth Starr	Paula White	Shirley Dobson
Political role	Preacher, politician, Jenny Craig endorser!	Lawyer.	Preacher.	Wife of Dr. James Dobson, and a woman concerned for America.
On any given day, he or she is . . .	Preparing next quote or sending apologies for quotes.	Still Googling Monica Lewinsky's name.	Getting her nails done at Ching's Nails.	Pressing refresh on the DrudgeReport.com.
One word often associated with him or her	Omnipresent.	Monica.	Blonde.	James.
In his or her perfect world . . .	West Hollywood would become an island.	The trial would have gone his way.	Her publicist would be getting her on *Fox News* a lot more often.	She would have married a world famous Christian psychologist and been worth millions. *D'oh! Silly me.*
If running for president, his or her campaign slogan might be . . .	A vote for me is a vote for God Almighty!	Monica, Monica, wherefore art thou, Monica?	American blondes have more fun! [Like totally hot and godly fun!]	A woman's place is in her home, so make my home the White House!
On his or her iPod you'd find . . .	"You Light Up My Life."	Fito Olivares' "Monica." [*Hey, it might be true.*]	Tony Robbins' motivational series!	Usher. [*It's her weakness.*]
Known for	Liberty University.	The Monica Lewinsky trial.	A big church in Florida.	Mrs. James Dobson and the National Day of Prayer.
Still relevant?	Thomas Road Baptist Church thinks so.	Gosh, no.	She thinks so.	Her husband is. Does that count?

But Wait! There's More to the Mix of Christianity and Politics!!!

Does there have to be a division? Does our loyalty to the kingdom of God have to come into conflict with our loyalty to the country of our political citizenship? The desire to bring those two into unity has been a dream of Christians throughout history. The Roman Empire, after a couple hundred years of on-and-off persecution of Christians, experienced a national conversion and turned into the Holy Roman Empire — a government that supposedly combined the best of both worlds. Political power and divine rule were joined, and the king ruled with the guidance and approval of the church. For Christians at the time, it must have seemed, well, perfect. Can you imagine being an illegal sect one minute, living in caves to escape being thrown to the lions, and then suddenly discovering that your sect had become the national religion? It would be like Hitler converting to Judaism in the middle of World War II.

And yet, somehow things backfired. One minute it was all divine rule and happy theocracy — and the next minute it was the Inquisition and the Crusades. [*Okay, so we skipped a little fast through history there, but you get the idea.*] The gradual spread of abuses and corruptions eventually led to the Protestant Reformation and to the establishment of a bunch of different separatist groups in the church [which would eventually be known as denominations]. One such group, the Puritans, became the seed of yet another attempt at theocracy—the creation of a new, biblically based government in an entirely new world.

America's Politics and the Bible

Everyone knows that America was founded by a group of people who were deeply spiritual and [for the most part] deeply Christian and that they came to America in search of religious freedom. But the truth is more, well, complicated. [Isn't it always?] For one thing, many of the Founding Fathers were not Puritans but Deists, and for them, political freedom was the real goal—but it was a goal that went hand in hand with religious freedom. For another thing, what the Puritans really meant by religious freedom was somewhat different from what we mean by it today. They didn't necessarily mean "the freedom for everyone to practice religion the way he or she wants to" but something more like "the freedom for us to practice religion the way we want to"—which, as I'm sure you'll agree, isn't exactly the same thing. [Actually, you could argue that it's exactly the opposite, but that's a different book.] Anyway, the Puritans were definitely not trying to establish a country tolerant of religious freedom [you read *The Crucible*, right?]. They were trying to establish God's kingdom on earth.

Like so many others before them, the Puritans were politicians just as much as [*you might even argue more than*] they were Christians.

Of course, the Puritans may have been the earliest colonists in the New World, but they weren't the ones who wrote the Constitution. The government that the United States ended up with was much closer to the ideas of tolerance and freedom than to the idea of a kingdom theocracy. Sure, many of the new nation's laws were based on the Ten Commandments, and most of the Founding Fathers believed that America was founded on divine principles. However, they weren't looking to create a theocracy, and they were a lot more likely to let their politics influence their theology than the other way around.

And yet in modern times the argument continues. There are still people who want the U.S. government to be completely based on biblical principles. There are others who want a government that's based entirely on personal freedom. And the idea of God's kingdom is still a dream that plenty of people want but nobody really understands.

So how should a Christian today be involved in politics? What party should you vote for? What position should you take on controversial political issues? Should you just give up on politics since the world sucks anyway? Should you try to get our country's laws to mimic the Ten Commandments? Or should you focus on building community with other Christians and being a good example to the world around you?

Sorry to disappoint you, but this book isn't going to answer those questions for you. Why not? Because we believe those are questions that, ultimately, you have to answer for yourself. [*Hey, individual choice is still the American way!*] And maybe there is no one right answer; maybe different Christians are supposed to do different things in the world of politics today. Maybe there's no right answer at all, and we as American Christians just have to choose the lesser of two evils [*I often feel that way on election day*]. Or maybe—maybe the right answer is one we haven't discovered yet. Maybe there's a good way to balance the tension between theology and politics, a way to influence the world without being influenced by it and to build God's kingdom without becoming corrupt. Maybe that way hasn't been done yet and you—the person reading this right now—are the one who will discover it and put it into practice.

The Politics of Jesus!?

Though not a politician, Jesus might be the most politically divisive individual in the world. Like I suggested earlier, just saying "Jesus is Lord" was seen as a political threat to some in the early days of Christianity. But what were the politics of Jesus? What would have been his slogan? Would he have supported health-care reform? How would he have viewed Hillary? Most of these questions can't be answered. Well, I take that back; I could answer them, but my answers would be based on theories and not truthful statements. [Though I'm quite sure he would have loved Hillary Clinton much like he loves me.] However, Jesus made some strong statements about society and how it should work. You shouldn't consider your politics without considering the words and passions of Jesus. Here are a few things you might want to learn, relearn, or at least read *before* you enter the voting booth.

First and foremost. Love God and love people. [*Jesus said these are the two greatest commandments!*] And guess what? These two commandments don't need to be hung up in the courthouse for validation. We just need to live them.

Beatitudes. In the fifth chapter of Matthew, Jesus lays out his idea of the kingdom — you know, words about being pure in heart, being peacemakers, and the importance of loving and seeking his truth. It might be good for you to read that again. [And *again* and *again*.]

Parables. Nearly every parable offers a unique perspective on life, one that could affect a person's politics. In the parables — the stories about the mustard seed, the prodigal son, the rich young ruler, and the pearl of great price — we learn about the passions and values of Jesus.

Miracles. The miracles Jesus performed showed his compassion for people. He always walked into people's lives and took care of their practical needs as well as their spiritual needs.

Conversations. Lastly, reread and reconsider the conversations Jesus had. Many of these conversations are chock-full of glimpses into his politics. I'm not sure we can read Jesus' interactions with Nicodemus, the woman at the well, and the Pharisees without considering how it could or should affect our politics.

The Issues

[everything we are concerned about]

It's pretty hard to find the right result to a controversial issue.

— Max Baucus

Welcome to the issues section. Usually I'm a big fan of issues! Yeah, I have a strange fetish for talking rather openly about my issues. But unfortunately, this section isn't about *my* issues. If so, you and I would be having a lot more fun right about now. But try to have fun. And smile. It wouldn't hurt you to just look pleasant while reading this little book. Gosh, even books about politics have feelings.

Well, not really.

As you might know, this book is part of a series, and when I started writing it, I really thought I already had the most difficult topics of the series behind me. I mean, what could be more controversial than sex? [*Just saying the word* sex *gets people fired up — in more ways than one.*] And Christianity and money are both pretty heavy topics, too. But I've discovered that in today's divided culture, the subject of politics might be an even bigger lightning rod for emotions and controversy. Even as I've been writing this book, nearly everyone I've come in contact with [*not that I come in contact with many people while I'm writing a book*] has been quick to offer his or her opinion. [*And seriously, people's opinions about politics are just as bizarre as their opinions about, well, you know.*]

BUT STILL, PEOPLE HAVEN'T BEEN ABLE TO RESIST OFFERING THEIR BEST ADVICE.

"I think you should write about all the good things James Dobson does," one lady told me. I looked at her seriously and assured her that James would make it into the book. "Please cover the issues surrounding homeschooling," said another. When I politely replied, "I'm not sure that topic affects enough people to be included in this book," she gave me a look that clearly showed she didn't care much for my response. A gay friend asked me if I would be talking about homosexuality, and I told him that because it's an issue that's debated in many political circles today, it would be addressed in the book. [Though honestly, I believe homosexuality shouldn't be a political issue. That's just my personal opinion. But you know, some people can make any topic a political one. And be vocal about it.]

I always thought politics was one of the topics you weren't supposed to talk about with strangers *or in public.* That and religion. Maybe it's just me, but it appears things have changed a lot these days. People seem much less afraid to voice their opinions and thoughts about politics. Hot topics like the war on terrorism, an amendment prohibiting gay marriage, and immigration often take precedence in discussions around the water cooler. [*Now, I know pop culture nonsense—like Paris Hilton, Jessica Simpson, and little baby Suri—still gets more attention, but we are more likely to talk about politics than in years past.*]

✪ ✪ ✪ ✪ ✪ ✪ ✪ ✪ ✪ ✪ ✪ ✪ ✪ ✪ ✪ ✪ ✪ ✪

So did I [L. C. Baker]. Apparently a lot of people think otherwise – especially if they think you might have the power to make their opinions known. I happened to mention to some person in Borders who was admiring my laptop that I was working on a book about politics, and before I knew it, I'd spent several hours discussing national health care and racism in America with a Sikh medical student from Canada. Which just goes to show you that nearly everybody – even people who aren't Americans – has an opinion about politics in the U.S. [*We'll get to that soon enough.*]

✪ ✪ ✪ ✪ ✪ ✪ ✪ ✪ ✪ ✪ ✪ ✪ ✪ ✪ ✪ ✪ ✪ ✪

Why do people feel comfortable talking about politics now? I think part of the reason is that we're more aware than we were in the past. News bombards our personal space on all fronts. We can't escape it; it's on our computers, phones, TVs, and radios. Also, news has become much more personal for Americans since 9/11. Before that day, news was a kind of virtual reality that we watched from the outside—something that happened somewhere else, in some other part of the world. Now we've been reminded firsthand how terribly and drastically news can affect us. We've experienced how the news can change our lives in an instant. And so we're a lot more concerned, a lot more informed, and a lot more passionate.

The issues that concern us today are not simple ones [*issues are never simple, really*]. Sometimes they divide us. Sometimes they unite us. But mostly they involve individual circumstances [stories and narratives] that are often difficult to understand [unless you've walked a similar path] and impossible to resolve without hurting another human being.

I know personally what issues can do.
[*And, no, I'm not talking about my personal issues.*]

I'll never forget November 4, 1992 — a presidential election day. [I was almost nineteen and had *almost* finished puberty — no really, *don't laugh*; it's a sensitive topic!] I was sad that day. In fact, after the results of the election were announced, I believed the world would soon be coming to an end. And it wasn't because Bill Clinton had been voted in as president. That was the least of my worries. Okay, that's a lie — it wasn't the *least* of my worries. Considering that I was about as right-winged as an elephant could be during that time, I thought for sure that a Clinton administration was going to take America to the toilet. [*And, yes, I admit it: I was wrong—well, sort of. The impeachment trials were certainly toiletesque.*] But that wasn't the main reason I was so unhappy. On election day 1992, I thought the world was coming to an end because my home state of Maryland had passed legislation that legalized partial-birth abortion.

The day after the election, I felt depressed and overwhelmed. I couldn't discuss the prior day's happenings without becoming emotional. That issue affected me. Yet partial-birth abortion is simply one of hundreds of issues that people like you and I become passionate about in America.

When it comes to the issues, people become passionate for different reasons. Some are concerned about the environment [*I love tree huggers!*]. Others are concerned that when we grow old, we will not have social security [*and we want our $587 a month!*]. Some of the issues we debate here in America are rather petty—*like whether or not we'll receive a $50 income tax cut next year.* Other issues are very serious; take for example the aforementioned *partial-birth abortion.* No matter what side of this issue you're on, you can't deny that it's a difficult issue to understand. And sadly, those who are in favor of it often have zero concept about what happens during the procedure. [*I know that's an opinion, but you can deal with me having one or two, right?*]

But despite the complexity of political issues, you can't run from them. You could try, but these issues are the heart and soul of politics, and a lot of them are the heart and soul of America [*for better or worse*]. The issues concerning America's culture, economy, foreign policy — every aspect of our lives — are the reasons we get off our butts on election day and stand in line at voting booths. Issues are powerful and influential; they're the reasons you dislike one candidate and love another. A politician's position on a single issue can make or break his or her candidacy for a voter — or even for his or her entire constituency. One bad vote on an important issue, and a Congresswoman could lose her next election.

And, as you know, America has a lot of issues. More seem to get added to the mix every day. In this section, we're going to focus on a number of core issues that most Americans have strong opinions about. And maybe a couple we should have strong opinions about.

So are you ready to jump in? Even if you think you are, parts of this section may make you mad. Let me give you some advice about how to begin learning about the topics that will be covered.

Pray [yes, get down on your knees and talk with God — *or just listen*]. First and foremost, as you begin to read about the following issues, ask God to give you wisdom and insight. Listen for God's Spirit to speak to you as you trek your way through these topics.

Have an open mind [*um, free your mind; okay, do it just a little*]. This book attempts to present both sides of the issues from a nonpartisan perspective. And no matter what your opinion, that is guaranteed to offend you at one point or another. So even if you believe you already know how to think about an issue, enter this conversation with a mind open enough to hear another side of the story. Remember, these issues affect people — real flesh-and-blood human beings. And remember, too, that we Christians are not here to wage war against people; people should never be our "issue."

Learn both sides [*or all ten sides*] **of an issue before making a decision.** One of the biggest mistakes many Christians make — whether Democrat or Republican — is failing to truly experience both sides of the issues and to listen to how others think about the "true picture" *before* making up their minds. There's little worse than people who make up their minds without studying the facts for themselves.

[Oh, and don't take someone else's opinion and make it your own just because you like that person — I know you like me, but still, don't do it!]

Your opinion doesn't have to be a destination [*it's okay to grow, change your mind, and then grow some more*]. All of us are in process. How you think and feel about an issue today might change five years down the road. So don't be too quick to SCREAM your opinion about an issue from the mountaintops. In other words, many laughed at the thought of global warming ten or fifteen years ago — *me included* — but many of those people aren't laughing anymore. In most cases, your opinions about the topics covered in this book are not "destinations" where you'll stand firm for the rest of your life [*nor should they be*]. Be willing to grow from each experience God puts you through; let God use the events in your life to educate you and make you more like him, *not* more like a particular party. We're not here to become *more* Republican or *more* Democrat or even *more* Green or *more* Libertarian; we're here to become more like Jesus.

Okay, now we can get started. Oh, one more thing! We've divided the issues into three groups: Our Society, Our World, and Our Future. Some, of course, affect all three.

 **NOW WE CAN GET STARTED.**

Truth to Know

And that about wraps it up. God is strong, and he wants you strong. So take everything the Master has set out for you, well-made weapons of the best materials. And put them to use so you will be able to stand up to everything the Devil throws your way. This is no afternoon athletic contest that we'll walk away from and forget about in a couple of hours. This is for keeps, a life-or-death fight to the finish against the Devil and all his angels.

Be prepared. You're up against far more than you can handle on your own. Take all the help you can get, every weapon God has issued, so that when it's all over but the shouting you'll still be on your feet.

(Ephesians 6:10-13)

The Issues That Affect Our Society
[the stuff that hits each of us
personally, but in different ways]

Let's talk about drugs.

I'm assuming you know what I mean by drugs, right? Yeah, of course you do. Lucky for us, in today's political scene, drugs are something that most candidates, whether conservative or liberal, can agree on. There are a few extreme liberals, mostly Libertarians and Green partiers [*and a couple librarians from the sixties and seventies — oh, you'd be surprised about some librarians*], who argue in favor of drug legalization. These prolegalization types argue that drugs are usually a victimless crime and if people want to destroy their bodies with drugs, then they should be allowed to do it. [*Yeah, let's hear it for self-mutilation! I'm kidding!*] Furthermore, they conclude that keeping drugs illegal is no different from the prohibition of alcohol in the early 1900s. [*And that was pretty silly!*]

However, the majority of candidates — both Republicans and Democrats — are in favor of keeping drugs illegal and of preventing and decreasing drug use in America. The biggest dividing line on the issue of drugs is not whether they should be legalized but rather how drug offenders should be handled [*i.e., punished, whipped, and shamed for their habits*].

Though we probably won't be voting on this topic anytime soon, one of the biggest issues today is simply TOO much information. When it comes to politics, not only can the information be addictive, time consuming, and mind numbing, but it can also sometimes keep us from the most important things, like living our lives in peace, contentment, and harmony with others. So take my advice. Sometimes it's necessary to:

- **Turn off _Fox News_ and CNN.** Too much television news will make an unhappy you!

- **Stop refreshing the DrudgeReport.com.** Yes, I know that Matt Drudge seems to get _all_ the news before it happens, but please, give yourself a break once in a while from getting the latest on war, politics, and Hillary.

- **Stop the e-mail news alerts.** At one time, I had more than six news alerts coming to my inbox. I couldn't check my e-mail without getting news about another tragedy around the world.

- **Schedule an information-free day at least once a month.** Take a break on all media for a day; I promise that Bill O'Reilly and Anderson Cooper will still be there the next day!

Now, it's not like I'm telling you to be uninformed; just don't be overconsumed with news and information — you'll thank me for this one!

On the more conservative side, the vanguard of the antidrug army argues for harsh punishments. This is the position that coined the phrase "the war on drugs." Yeah, you might remember Nancy Reagan's "Just Say No!" campaign — it was a huge success, and that's why drugs are hardly an issue these days! [Yes, I'm being sarcastic!] This position

wants to destroy drug use through harsher sentences, enforced imprisonment, and getting people off the streets — basically through any means necessary. On the side of prevention, they especially want to punish dealers and other people who get new users started on drugs.

A more moderate position focuses more on punishing suppliers than on punishing users. Moderate conservatives usually focus on stopping drug shipments from crossing the border and on bringing down drug cartels and suppliers. They are also enthusiastic users of the phrase "the war on drugs."

A more moderate liberal position focuses on prevention rather than on punishment. This position wants to reduce demand through treatment programs and drug education. Instead of enacting harsh punishments on people who are already users, this position wants to focus efforts on preventing more people from becoming users. It advocates focusing efforts on at-risk populations and understanding the causes of drug use in order to prevent it before it begins.

The most extreme liberals, as I already mentioned, want to legalize drugs. Some argue for legalized medical use of drugs like marijuana [which is currently legal for medical use in twelve states[1]]. Melissa Etheridge swore by it for pain during chemotherapy.

FACT: In 2003, it was believed that 6.2 percent of individuals twelve or older had used marijuana in the past month.[2] That equaled nearly fifteen million people. In contrast, only 119,000 used heroin.[3]

The phrase "the war on drugs" was first used by President Nixon in 1971; two years earlier he had described drug abuse as "America's public enemy number one."[4] [*Obviously he wasn't including dishonest politicians on that list.*] In the seventies, the depressed economies in Latin America combined with the "sex, love, and drugs" hippie movement in the United States to create a growing supply of drugs from Latin America and a growing demand in the United States.

The Office of National Drug Control Policy was founded under Reagan in 1988. The ONDCP basically coordinates all the antidrug programs run by the federal government, from passing laws to researching the effects of drugs on users and society. The most fun fact about the ONDCP is that the official title of its director is Drug Czar. Sounds kind of like a mafia title, which, depending on your politics, may or may not be appropriate for the guy who pretty much heads up the war on drugs.

FACT: In 2002, about 1.5 million drug-related arrests were made.[5]

Almost half of the drug arrests in the U.S. today are related to marijuana, which is another reason some politicians advocate its legalization. I guess that would be one way to win the war on drugs: just declare a victory and move out. [*And it would make Dave Matthews fans everywhere jump up and down with glee!*]

An additional consideration when debating the legalization of at least some of the "lighter" drugs, such as marijuana, is prison overcrowding. The United States has the largest prison population in the world, and 55 percent of federal inmates are there for drug-related crimes.[6]

Finally, drugs are closely tied with border and international issues, especially with Latin America. Most of the U.S.'s drug supply comes from Latin America, and it is usually shipped across the Mexican border. Proponents of the drug war, therefore, are also very concerned about protecting the border and preventing drug imports.

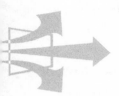

FACT: Citing a September 19, 2006, report on drug prevention, NBC's *Today* show reported that America's antidrug commercials were ineffective in the fight against illegal drug use.

Consider These Points When Thinking About the Issue of Legalizing Drugs

☒ First, are you a drug user [*or would you like to be*]?

☒ If you're not a user, do you think it's okay for people to use drugs as long as they're not hurting anyone else?

☒ Do you think drugs are a health problem? How should laws prevent drug use?

☒ Do you think that anyone who uses drugs is just an idiot who makes bad choices? What kinds of laws and punishments should be enforced for drug use?

Personal Opinions

▨ "I am not a drug user, but I do believe that legalizing marijuana for medical purposes would be a good thing." *Dee, 29*

▨ "I have a brother who is a drug addict. And so after seeing what the drugs have done in his life, I'm in favor of harsh sentences against people who bring drugs into this country illegally." *Sean, 24*

Three Questions to Consider

1 Have you been personally affected by drugs? Has that experience altered your political view of drugs? If so, how?

2 Would you ever be *in favor* of legalizing all or some drug use? Why or why not?

3 What do you believe is the biblical perspective of illegal drug use?

Crime: Take a bite out of it.

Okay, so in a way, crime is less controversial than most political issues. Unlike most issues that have supporters to the furthest extreme on both sides of the argument, just about everyone can agree that crime is bad. We all want less of it.

[Yay! 🖲 Something we can agree on!]

However, there's a lot of disagreement on the details, such as what, exactly, should be considered criminal [*is jaywalking really a crime?*] and how crimes should be dealt with when they occur [*should jaywalkers go to jail?*]. Think about these questions as they relate to crime:

Yay for New York City!

Although crime all over the U.S. began to fall in 1991, the city that reigns unchallenged as having the most improved crime rate is undoubtedly New York. Since 1991, New York City has experienced a 75 percent decrease in violent crime, giving it a 2006 crime rate that is lowest of the twenty-five largest cities in America. The New York drop in crime is often credited to the New York Police Department's crime analysis method, CompStat, which maps crime in city precincts and holds officers accountable for crime in their regions. However, CompStat was not implemented until 1994 after crime rates had already begun to drop, and other cities that have started similar programs have experienced varying rates of success.

- Should more or fewer potentially criminal actions—smoking marijuana, for instance—be illegal?
- Should criminals be punished more or less severely than they are now?
- Should the death penalty exist at all, and how much should it be enforced?
- What rights should convicted criminals have? And do changes need to be made to our criminal justice system?
- Most of all, how can we best prevent crime from happening in the first place?

Politicians fall all across the spectrum when it comes to determining what constitutes a crime. A politician's stance on whether or not a particular action should be considered a crime is as much a function of the topic as it is of conservatism or liberalism. For example, the donkeys are more likely to want owning a gun to be a crime and less likely to want recreational drug use to be illegal. The elephants, in general, are more likely to want the opposite. Members of the Green Party and Libertarian Party are usually in favor of making criminal as few actions as possible because they tend to favor very little government involvement in individuals' lives.

So what about crime prevention?

That question is the most important and the hardest to answer. It's important because it's the one thing about the issue that all politicians agree on: *Less crime makes for a happier America! More crime makes us all scared little puppy dogs afraid to go out our front doors.* But it's difficult to answer because so many factors influence crime that it's hard to pinpoint which factors successfully contribute to lowering the incidents of crime.

[Duh.]

In the 1980s, violent crime was rising at unprecedented rates all over the country, and sociologists predicted that it would continue to rise indefinitely. In 1991, nationwide crime rates suddenly—and inexplicably—dropped, and although they've gone up and down ever since, the overall trend has been decreasing. The weird thing is that no one really knows why. Theorists have cited policing strategies, economic improvements, government spending, the war on drugs, and even [most controversially] more abortions as the reasons behind the drop

Death-Penalty Debate: America's Flaw?!?

One of the more politically explosive topics connected with the issue of crime is the question of capital punishment. [*Should we do it? Or should we not do it?*] More than half of the countries in the world have abolished capital punishment entirely, and only sixty-nine countries still use the death penalty. The majority of executions take place in just four countries: China, Iran, Saudi Arabia, and the United States [94 percent in 2005].[7] Obviously, our use of the death penalty puts us in a worldwide minority, as well as putting us in company that, in the political realm, we'd generally rather avoid. However, supporters insist that use of the death penalty deters crime better than gentler methods.

in crime. But the fact remains that no one can point inarguably toward a single cause, which means that if crime were to begin rising again, we wouldn't have a definitely effective recourse for preventing it. And that means that the goal of lowering and preventing crime remains firmly in the realm of debate and therefore of politicians.

Various groups argue for different methods:

* **Liberals** tend to argue for preventative rather than punitive action and turn toward improving the economy, education, and youth programs to prevent the *creation* of criminals.

* **Conservatives** usually lean more toward "big stick" [*and I'm making no innuendo*] methods like tougher punishments for criminals, bigger police forces, and broken-windows policing that addresses even minor law infractions and quality-of-life issues, as well as major incidents.

Three Questions to Consider

1 What are your personal feelings regarding the use of the death penalty? If you're for it, how do you reconcile it with God's saying, "Vengeance is mine" (Hebrews 10:26)? And if you're against it, what are your thoughts about the Old Testament's practice of "an eye for an eye" (Exodus 21:24, NLT)?

2 What are some ways you can help your community actively reduce crime?

3 Name a few "sins" of our culture that you believe shouldn't be considered crimes.

Why Are You Against the Death Penalty?

☐ "I think the Bible teaches us to value life, and if I'm going to be against abortion, I should be against the death penalty." *John, 22*

☐ "It's not the government's place to punish a man or woman with death; I believe they should be locked away, but not put to death." *Geoffrey, 27*

☐ "God says, 'Vengeance is mine.' Period." *Jennifer, 24*

☐ "Who said I was against the death penalty?" *Helen, 29*

Gun Control: Should we sling 'em or shun 'em?

[by L. C. Baker]

On Tuesday, April 20, 1999, I was working as a teacher's assistant at a high school in Annandale, Virginia. Probably because I was working at a high school, the tragedy of Columbine—though half a country away—was, for me, terribly close to home. In the wake of the tragedy, we teachers were warned to be alert to the possibility of copycat violence. One of my students was expelled for calling in a bomb threat—which, admittedly, turned out to be fake, and he was easily caught since (a) he called from the pay phone just outside the campus police office and (b) the front-office secretary, whom he called to tell about the "bomb," recognized his voice because he'd been in the front office so many times for getting kicked out of class. Okay, so the closest our school came to a copycat threat was more like an episode of *Stupid Criminals*. But still, it was a frightening time. For months, I woke up every day wondering—wondering if something terrible would happen that day, wondering what awful news I hadn't heard yet. That's the impact that a national tragedy has on the individual psyche. Now let's talk.

 In the wake of the Columbine school shooting, moderate and liberal politicians jumped to respond with a long list of gun-control laws. It's an old argument in American politics: Gun-related crimes could be decreased and prevented if there were fewer guns available to criminals. The thinking is this:

◙ Guns are violent.
◙ The reason people want guns is to do something violent.

- Accidents happen with guns, especially with children.
- Gun accidents often mean that people get killed.
- Law-abiding adults who have guns don't adequately protect their children from accessing those guns.
- Guns are just plain dangerous, so let's get rid of them.

The other side of the argument, headed up, of course, by the good people at the NRA, is founded not in fear but in a constitutional amendment. The second amendment to the Constitution guarantees American citizens the "right to bear arms"—the right to own guns. And not just for hunting, either; the amendment actually talks about a "well-regulated militia," indicating that the guns it's referring to are military guns.

Of course, in the eighteenth century when the amendment was written, the United States, like many nations, didn't have a standing army to the extent that we have today. In times of war, civilians were not only allowed but expected to go to war and defend their homes—not necessarily by joining the standing army but by joining the civilian militia and becoming temporary soldiers. That's rarely, if ever, the purpose of owning guns today, but the intent behind owning guns is the same. Many gun owners want guns for hunting, but many others want them for self-defense so that they will be able to use force effectively if a burglar or other violent criminal attacked their home. Guns make people who have them and know how to use them feel safer; they know they can defend themselves if the need arises.

This just in — from down under.

The question then becomes whether having a gun does in fact deter crime. The old argument says that if guns are illegal, then only criminals will have guns. When Australia enacted stringent antigun laws following a gun-related crime in 1996, the NRA published a plethora of startling statistics demonstrating that violent crime, especially gun-related crime, in Australia had increased significantly after the enforcement of the ban. The Australian government protested, saying that the statistics were inaccurate. In reality, the statistics are probably inconclusive. Does gun control decrease violent crime? The answer often depends more on one's political persuasion than on the facts [*like it does with most everything*].

 But here are some of the facts anyway — according to each side.

First, from the Gun Owners Association

✳ "Guns are used 2.5 million times a year in self-defense"—that's over six thousand times a day. [*Now, I don't know where these events are happening, but that's what they say!*]

❋ "Concealed carry laws have reduced murder and crime rates in the states that have enacted them." [*But I must admit that the supporting stats for this claim are pretty low.*]

❋ "Twice as many children are killed playing football in school than are murdered by guns."[8] [*Hmm. Might want to rethink letting my kid join the team—when I have a kid, of course.*]

Now, from the Other Side, The Brady Bill Peeps

- "In 2000, more than nine young people aged 19 and under were killed a day in gun homicides, suicides and unintentional shootings in the United States." [*No support was given for this information.*]
- "A gun kept in the home is 22 times more likely to be used in an unintentional shooting (4 times), a criminal assault or homicide (7 times), or an attempted or completed suicide (11 times) than to be used to injure or kill in self-defense." [*Is this an obvious stat or what?*]
- "In 2000, suicide by all means took the lives of 29,350 people in the United States: of this number, 57% (16,586) were completed using a firearm."[9]

Now you decide which side of the issue you're on.

Three Questions to Consider

1 Were you raised in a gun-friendly environment? In other words, did your parents own guns?

2 Have you been personally affected by the use of firearms?

3 Should Americans have the right to bear arms? Why or why not?

Civil Rights and Homosexuality

Until 1973, homosexuality was officially considered a psychiatric condition. The *Diagnostic and Statistical Manual of Mental Disorders* published by the American Psychiatric Association used to list homosexuality as a mental disorder. However, in 1973, homosexuality officially became an acceptable lifestyle, at least from a psychological perspective. That was the first major victory for the gay, lesbian, and bisexual civil rights movement.

Using the language of civil rights to talk about homosexuality was a bold move in an age when homosexuality was widely viewed as a disease. Today society as a whole is increasingly coming to view homosexuals as another minority group, right next to African Americans, Latinos, and other ethnic groups. However, the validity of that view, and how much it ought to affect laws and society, continues to be a major political divide.

Two Sides When It Comes to the Gay, Lesbian, Bisexual, and Transgender Community

As I'm sure you're aware, liberal and conservative parties follow traditional lines when it comes to this issue: The conservatives support preserving the past, while the liberals desire change [*hence the reason they're called conservatives and liberals*]. Republicans tend to be against the passing of laws that protect homosexuals as a minority group or give them specific rights; Democrats, Libertarians, and Greens are in favor of such laws. Liberals argue that homosexuals are no different from any other minority group and deserve the same protection, while conservatives argue that homosexuality is an aberration or a sin and should not be recognized by political groups.

One of the Main Issues
[from a political standpoint]

For many people, the debate hinges on whether homosexuality is an innate condition or a personal choice. If it is a genetically determined condition, then discriminating against the homosexual lifestyle is no different from discriminating against different races. If it is a choice, however, there is no reason to treat it as a natural condition, and society has the right to reject it as an unacceptable lifestyle.

Gay Gene

[is there proof?]

Scientific studies on the question of whether or not homosexuality is genetically determined have been inconclusive at best. Generally, the study groups are too small or the evidence too scanty for scientists to say with certainty whether there is a genetic component to sexual behavior. One study, for example, showed a higher genetic correlation for divorce rates than for homosexuality. Another study seemed to have found a correlation between a certain area of the brain and homosexuality, but since that study involved deceased adult men, there was no way to determine whether the brain changes were causes or results of a homosexual lifestyle. A third study was widely touted as having found the "gay gene," the genetic marker for homosexuality. But the correlation between the gene and homosexual behavior was not absolute. No matter what activist groups on both sides of the argument claim, at this point there is not sufficient evidence for scientists to say whether or not — or to what extent — genetics influence homosexuality.[10]

Gay Marriage

[here comes the groom?]

One of the biggest political debates surrounding the issue of homosexual rights is the question of marriage. Liberal groups push on both the state and federal levels for the granting of more rights to gays in civil unions and for the legalization of gay marriage. The push for the latter has led to a reciprocal push on the conservative side in favor of a marriage amendment to the Constitution—either the U.S. Constitution or, failing that, to state constitutions. A marriage amendment would legally define marriage as a contract between a man and a woman, thus making the legalization of gay marriage impossible.

Right now, the question of homosexual marriage has been determined at the state level: Some states allow it, others don't. States that don't allow gay marriage are not required to legally recognize marriages that were performed in other states. Obviously, such a divided situation is not tenable long-term; in a united country, there will eventually have to be a united position on an issue that affects culture and society so deeply. And so the debate continues to rage.

Gays, Lesbians, and Adoption

Another hot topic surrounding the issue of homosexuality is adoption. Several states already allow homosexual couples to adopt children, but conservatives continue to resist that. They argue that children need the care of both genders, a mother and a father, to be successful in life, and they view the agenda of homosexual lobbyist groups as a threat to traditional families.

 Many conservatives feel that homosexual adults should never be placed in a position where they could influence children. This was evidenced on the political scene in the Supreme Court case *Boy Scouts of America v. Dale* (2000), in which the Boy Scouts successfully sued for the right to dismiss a gay scoutmaster.

The Christian Response

Among Christians, the issue of homosexuality is equally dividing. Evangelicals and fundamentalists look at passages in the Bible that mention homosexuality in a list of sins that believers are to avoid and interpret them literally, arguing that any homosexual relations are always sinful. But more liberal mainline denominations argue that those passages are culturally restricted, perhaps referring to the homosexual practices of pagan religions, and do not apply to homosexual couples in committed, monogamous relationships. Several denominations allow practicing homosexuals to be ordained as pastors, and some churches have performed marriage ceremonies for gay couples, ceremonies that are recognized by the church, although they are not legally binding.

Three Questions to Consider

1 This will be a difficult question for some of you: Should Christians [or conservatives] be able to control the freedoms of others who do not adhere to their belief system?

2 How would giving gays and lesbians the freedom to marry change marriage for men and women?

3 Is there a difference between a gay family adopting a child and a single mother or father raising a child?

Helping America's Poor

Poverty is an epidemic in America. Although we are one of the richest nations in the world, it is estimated that 3.5 million people in America experience homelessness each year.[11] The American dream is working for only a select few; for many American citizens, it

The Church Steps In!

As federal funding to welfare and aid programs has been cut, churches and other faith-based charitable organizations have begun to pick up some of the slack. This, of course, has a politically divisive side effect. Currently, the federal government supports the poverty-aid programs of faith-based organizations indirectly by offering tax incentives to people who donate to these organizations. Since all of a church's funding comes from donations, tax incentives should increase giving and therefore increase the budget that a church has to provide programs to help those in need. However, some groups feel that churches and other faith-based organizations should be able to receive federal grants for programs they are providing to help the poor and the homeless. Some advocacy groups support Charitable Choice, which would decrease the restrictions that prevent faith organizations from receiving federal money and enable churches to apply for federal grants to support their poverty-related programs. However, opponents feel that decreasing those restrictions would be a violation of the separation of church and state.

is a nightmare. Because the causes of poverty are so diverse and widespread, there is a wide variety of solutions offered by different groups.

	Liberals	Conservatives
The overview	In general, liberal parties tend to favor legislation that helps poor people by giving them money in some fashion — through federal or state programs that provide aid to people in need.	In general, conservative parties tend to prefer programs that help the needy through temporary aid and work-related programs.
The backstory	Liberals are usually much more willing to put money into aid and welfare programs than conservatives are.	Conservatives tend to see poverty as a personal problem of the individual, a result of someone's refusal to work or untreated mental illness.
The theme	Liberals are more likely to view poverty as a problem of society that society as a whole is responsible for helping to cure.	Conservatives prefer to cut funding to welfare programs in order to reduce taxes or reduce deficit.

Some Recent History in the Fight to Help America's Needy

☆ In 1996, President Clinton passed a welfare reform law that moved programs for needy families and individuals under the direction of states and out of the provision of federal programs.

☆ Temporary Aid for Needy Families (TANF), a federal grant, helps fund state programs, creates strict requirements that recipients must be working, and also puts a strict time limit on how long a particular family or individual can receive funds.

☆ Food stamps, another major federally funded program, are intended to supplement the money a household is able to spend on food up to the amount needed for the USDA's Thrifty Food Plan (TFP).

☆ Other government programs that help low-income families are HUD housing programs. Legislation was passed in 1999 that combined several previous programs into the housing choice vouchers program.

Other Issues to Consider

✖ In recent years, homeless people have become the targets of hate crimes and prejudice, and many believe they should therefore be protected under federal law.

✖ The federal minimum wage is another issue that must be thought about. Barbara Ehrenreich explores the insufficiency of the minimum wage to support even a single working person in her book *Nickel and Dimed: On (Not) Getting By in America*. Ehrenreich attempted to support herself by working minimum-wage jobs and discovered that it just isn't possible — even for a well-educated white woman — to pay rent and buy food while making minimum wage.

✖ Finally, health care is often simply unaffordable for low-income families. However, it is an essential issue to address when considering the problems of poverty because much of the problem of homelessness in America would be eliminated with adequate health care.

Three Questions to Consider

1 As followers of Jesus, what are our responsibilities to those who are less fortunate?

2 Do you think our modern political practices for the poor are working or making matters worse?

3 Which political party—from your perspective—has the better plan to reduce poverty?

Abortion—The Deal Breaker for So Many Christians

For a good number of Christians, abortion is the central issue in the American political scene today—and has been since 1973, when *Roe v. Wade* was passed by the Supreme Court. Even "crunchy cons" and "closet liberals" tend to draw the line when it comes to abortion. Derek Webb, a Christian musician who has become increasingly involved in the political scene and has affiliated himself more and more with progressives, was once asked in an interview—in the midst of espousing "leftist" policies like debt forgiveness for Third World countries—whether he could ever vote for a candidate who supported abortion. His response? Absolute silence.

The biblical basis for the pro-life argument has been vigorously and repeatedly defended in hundreds of venues, from books and articles to political brochures. Put simply, the pro-life position is that a life is a life, and God is the Creator and defender of life. He is the defender of the weak and helpless, from widows and orphans to unborn babies. He is the protector of the innocent, and who could be more innocent than a baby in the womb? Life begins at conception, and from the moment life is created, the destruction of that life is murder. An unborn baby, from the moment of conception, is an individual created by God with a soul and a future, and to kill that soul is an act of murder and a terrible sin. It is comparable to the heathen practice of sacrificing children to idols—in abortion, children are sacrificed to the idols of free sex and individual hedonism. Through abortion, a mother willfully murders her child—the worst kind of murder imaginable.

In the modern political landscape, pro-choice Christians are hard to find. It is the abortion issue, more than any other, that has painted the dividing line between red and blue, assuring that almost everyone who identifies with Christ or with biblical values is firmly planted on the right side of the line. [*But* ...]

But is there something to be said for the other side? Well, *maybe.*

For one thing, there are a lot of problems with the absolute pro-life position. Pro-lifers tend to be shockingly short-sighted. The easiest argument here is special cases; the ones usually listed are rape, incest, and protecting the life of the mother when it is endangered. The extreme pro-life position forbids abortion in any situation, but clearly it's not a difficult argument to say, from the perspective of justice and righteousness, that a woman who was raped shouldn't have to bear the child of her rapist. Similarly, in a situation where it's a choice between the life of the unborn child and the life of the mother, who is also [for example] a wife and the mother of two other young children, it's not difficult to argue, from an ethical perspective, that it's better for the family to sacrifice the unborn child.

Another skeleton in the closet for the hard-line pro-life position is the absence of support for anything [other than abstinence] that would prevent abortions. *Nobody likes abortion!* Can I say that again? *NOBODY LIKES ABORTION!* Most pro-choice advocates agree that abortions should be safe, legal, and *rare*. One of the best ways to make abortions rare is by encouraging the use of birth control. But the hard-line pro-life position is usually also opposed to making birth control and sex education available. The reason, of course, is that extreme pro-lifers are often not just against abortion — they're also against sex. Okay, so they might be in favor of marital sex, although sometimes I wonder. [If you'd ever met the youth director from my old church, then you'd understand!] But in the minds of Christians, premarital sex is a big no-no, and so many pro-lifers strongly discourage the use of any form of birth control because, well, you shouldn't be having sex in the first place unless you want to have a baby.

Obviously, abstinence is the best form of prevention. But clearly, if abstinence is not happening, another form of prevention would be better than the terrible cure of abortion. I fully understand the argument that passing out condoms in schools is tantamount to giving kids permission to have sex. How far kids are willing to go is heavily influenced by the expectations that are placed on them. But it's the parents, not the government, who form those expectations, and obviously [though unfortunately] there are a lot of parents out there who *expect* their children to have sex before they're married. That's not something the government can change. So doesn't it make sense to at least offer birth control as an option? Surely there's some kind of middle ground of prevention that could keep families involved without deliberately cutting kids off from preventative measures that could keep them from ever being in a position where abortion is a consideration.

There are many Christian churches that do support the right to choose abortion as a right that's essential to religious

 freedom. For one thing, many Christians feel that giving the government the right to dictate when and whether a woman should have a baby is a form of religious persecution. Having a baby is a decision with personal, moral, social, and spiritual implications. And so, many Christians argue, it's a decision that should be made not by the government but by the woman and the man involved, with the support and prayers of their family and church.

A government that tries to dictate such moral decisions is trying to play God, and it's simply not the government's place.

Furthermore, as Christians we must consider issues of justice, health, and safety—for the woman and families involved as well as for the unborn—surrounding the question of abortion. Is it a wise, godly decision for a fifteen-year-old girl, the child of poor working parents, to bring another life into their family? What if her family simply won't be able to feed another child? What if she knows her child will be born with serious health or physical defects and is therefore unlikely to be adopted? Obviously, the best decision would have been for her to not get pregnant, but once she is, she might be forced to choose the lesser of two evils.

Can abortion ever be the lesser evil? Many churches believe so. The Episcopal Church issued a statement saying that "legislation concerning abortions will not address the root of the problem. . . . Any proposed legislation . . . must take special care to see that the individual conscience is respected, and that the responsibility of individuals to reach informed decisions in this matter is acknowledged and honored."[12] The Presbyterian Church (USA) made a statement that, while expressing concern that abortion should not be used as a convenience or to "ease embarrassment," said, "the considered decision of a woman to terminate a pregnancy can be a morally acceptable, though certainly not the only or required, decision." The PC (USA) also urged Christians to "address the circumstances that bring a woman to consider abortion as the best available option. Poverty, unjust social realities, sexism, racism, and inadequate supportive relationships may render a woman virtually powerless to choose freely."[13] And The United Methodist Church put out a statement in 2004 that, while rejecting abortion as birth control or for gender selection, issued a call to "all Christians to a searching and prayerful inquiry into the sorts of conditions that may warrant abortion" and stated the Christian responsibility "to respect the sacredness of the life and well-being of the mother, for whom devastating damage may result from an unacceptable pregnancy."[14]

As with any other political issue, there's no single clear answer to the problem of abortion. Listen to both sides and prayerfully consider all situations before you make your own decision about where you stand on this extremely controversial and moral issue.

Three Questions to Consider

1 If you are pro-life, could you ever vote for someone who was pro-choice? If you are pro-choice, could you ever vote for someone who was pro-life?

2 Have you had a personal experience with abortion, perhaps because of a friend or family member's choice to have an abortion? How has that experience affected you?

3 Would you ever be in favor of birth control in schools if it was proven to reduce the abortion rate?

The Issues That Affect Our World

American Foreign Policy

[by L. C. Baker]

I'd always heard that Europeans don't like Americans. Maybe it's because we talk too loud; maybe it's because we're taller and larger; maybe it's just because we look funny in our white socks. So the first time I traveled to Europe, I expected that strangers would tend to dislike me for being American. I thought I'd have to earn their trust by proving that I'm not like the usual tourist. However, I learned—as is so often the case—that the stereotype doesn't always hold true. I'm sure there are plenty of places in Europe [France, maybe?] where the old prejudices still stick. But in Eastern Europe, in Romania, and in all the old communist countries I visited, the common stereotype is exactly the opposite from reality.

"You're American?!" Romanian teenagers would ask me in awe. "What's it like to live in America? What kind of music do you like—do you like Madonna? Have you ever been in a movie? And have you ever met the Backstreet Boys?"

To the Romanians I met, we Americans are movie stars, exotic creatures from another world where the streets are [at least figuratively] made of gold and everyone is as rich as Midas. Most Romanian teens could dream of nothing better than to go to America. They'll gladly fake passports and sneak across borders in the hope of someday making it to America for a better life. And if they ever do make it, they won't look back. In Romania, as in most of formerly communist Europe, America is the dream of the West, a place where anything can happen and where dreams always come true, where everyone is rich and everything is just like it is on television.

Great. That's the perfect way to perceive America.

So there's at least one part of the world that still likes us. And that's all well and good—but what's it got to do with foreign policy?

 From our perspective, the constant export—mostly through Hollywood—of our culture, life-styles, and beliefs [with varying levels of accuracy] has nothing to do with our military or economic policies. But from the perspective of other countries all over the world, the ubiquitous presence of our culture goes hand in hand with our foreign policy. And whether we want to be or not, America is everywhere. Although we call the sending of our stuff all over the world globalization, the plain fact is that it's mostly Americanization. It's American culture that's being exported, for better or worse, and everything we do today in foreign policy, whether military, economic, or political, happens in the wake of a wave of culture that has already gone ahead of us.

Today the United States has diplomatic relations with almost every country in the world. The few that we don't have relations with directly or officially [like Cuba] we manage to have connections with indirectly, usually through neutral third parties. [Sort of like the way you might have handled an argument when you were in fourth grade: "I'm not speaking to you!" "I'm not speaking to you either!" "Tell him I'm mad at him!" "Tell her I'm mad back!" Okay, so it's not exactly like that, but it's close.] But exactly what kind of policies we're pursuing, what our motivations are, and how much we should be intervening in situations overseas continues to be a matter of hot debate.

In today's politics, those who desire isolationism [a government policy based on the belief that national interests are best served by avoiding economic and political alliances with other countries[15]] tend to be, surprisingly, the more liberal political groups. Why? Because some argue that the current U.S. policies amount to imperialism. What are the main complaints?

- ▦ We set up and take down governments as we see fit. [*We do that sometimes.*]
- ▦ We intervene with sovereign nations in disputes that are none of our business. [*But come on, only when there's oil at stake.*]
- ▦ We think we're the policemen of the world [*Again, only for OPEC countries and Israel.*]
- ▦ We have our noses in other people's business.

Those who criticize this form of foreign policy also question the motives, pointing out that we don't interfere in all dictatorial governments or all governments that violate human rights, only

in the ones that are also violating our economic or political interests. So, for example, we don't care if Saudi Arabia is a tyrannical monarchy because they are nice to us and give us all the oil we want; it's only Iraq that bothers us because they don't like us and don't want to give us oil.

The opposing position, usually held by more conservative groups, argues that American foreign policy has always, or nearly always, been motivated and guided by benevolent desires. As Spiderman says, with great power comes great responsibility. The United States, as one of the only remaining world superpowers, has the responsibility to protect weaker nations from tyranny and to encourage the spread of democracy and freedom. For us to stand idly by and watch as tyrants invade and oppress other nations would be the same as an individual watching a woman being raped and doing nothing. We have a responsibility to the world to help keep the peace and to make the world a better place.

Both sides have good arguments; both want the United States to be an agent of good and of peace in the world. They just disagree about the way this should be achieved.

Three Questions to Consider

1 To what extent do you think America should be involved in other countries?

2 Do you think the United States has the right to impose democracy in other parts of the world? If so, in what circumstances?

3 Do you think American foreign policy is self-interested?

Terrorism

Here's a bit of irony. Of course, some would argue that it's not irony at all—just a coincidence, they'd say—but interestingly enough, I'm writing these words on September 12, five years and one day after the most horrific terrorist attack on American soil. It would have been more impressive if I'd written it yesterday, but, well, I couldn't write yesterday about the politics of terrorism. It didn't feel right. And I was too busy trying not to cry at the memories.

**[Matt Lauer and the cast of the
Today show like to make me cry. 😢]**

 It's strange to think that someday, someone might be reading this book who doesn't remember 9/11 as a vivid and terrible event of his or her life. Someone might be reading this who didn't experience that day as his or her personal Rubicon, the dividing line between a world that was safe and a world that is no longer. [Okay, so my hopes for this book may be WAY too high.]

In the five years since 9/11, terrorism has become a central issue in the political realm. A topic that once had more to do with history and world events came home to the United States that day, and it's been here ever since. After the attack five years ago, the United States was more united, within herself and with her allies, than she'd been in living memory. Now, the red and blue states are a symbol of the divisiveness of politics. It's sad to think that something as terrible as terrorism could be used not only as a physical weapon by enemies but as a political weapon within the U.S.

How does terrorism affect politics?

The big questions are these: Are Americans safe on domestic soil? What about on foreign soil? Where might a terrorist try to strike next? What does our intelligence tell us is their next target? And what can we do to make America more safe?

On the radio yesterday, I heard a survey cited showing that a majority of Americans believe terrorists will attack again. Every day since 9/11, surveys have shown that Americans expect an imminent attack—usually within the next ninety days. Since 9/11, the political debate has never been about whether or not the attacks might come. It's only been about the best way to defend against them.

Supporters of the most aggressive war on terror, usually conservatives and even some moderates, want the strictest measures possible enforced to protect American soil. They want the borders tightened and security measures increased. They welcome the Patriot Act and other laws that allow monitoring of terrorists and suspects, even if it means monitoring a lot of innocents as well. They are sometimes seemingly more concerned about safety than about civil or personal rights. They believe that we are engaged in a war, and they are willing to live under wartime conditions, sacrificing some personal freedoms for the sake of better security.

Opponents also believe that a terrorist attack might be imminent, but they are not willing to limitlessly sacrifice personal freedoms for the sake of protection. They want to keep limits on the government's power to monitor, question, and arrest suspects. They want to ensure that innocent people do not give up civil rights for the sake of catching terrorists. They want to balance the danger with the freedom that is essential to the very essence and identity of America. They don't want to become just like the enemy in order to defeat him.

The war on the home front is a war of protection, of civil liberties versus security measures. But that's just the defensive piece of the war on terror. Terrorism is not a domestic issue, and the most controversial piece of the war is the part that we're waging abroad.

Bush didn't coin the phrase "war on terror"; it was first used in the 1800s in discussions of anarchist movements. However, George W. gave the phrase a new meaning. Just days after the 9/11 attacks, he made a speech in which he stated his determination to "seek out terror wherever we find it" and destroy it at home and abroad. To that end, he led the U.S. military in attacks first on Afghanistan and then on Iraq.

The operation in Afghanistan met little opposition at the time. It was an offense against the ruling Taliban, based on intelligence that the Taliban had supported and was harboring the terrorists who orchestrated the 9/11 attacks. Although the operation failed to capture the terrorists, most notably Osama bin Laden, the primary target, it did succeed in overthrowing the Taliban. At the time, conservatives and liberals were united in the feeling that something had to be done, and quickly, in response to the attacks.

After overthrowing the Taliban in Afghanistan, Bush turned to Iraq and Saddam Hussein as the next harbor of terrorists that would be attacked. It was this move that brought to the surface controversy over foreign policy in the war on terror. Opponents felt that the connection between Iraq and 9/11 was sketchy, if not nonexistent. On this issue, opponents and supporters are very much divided along party lines, with most Republicans feeling that the operation in Iraq is an essential part of the war on terror and most Democrats feeling it is not. Interestingly, this is a case in which the language one uses is a clear indicator of his or her politics. Politicians who support the operation in Iraq, considering it an important step in fighting terrorism in the world, refer to the military operation there as the "war on terror." Politicians who consider Iraq an unnecessary offensive refer to it as the "war in Iraq."

The biggest question in Iraq, which will continue to be an issue should the conflict extend to other countries as well, is whether preemptive strikes are a valid means of

deterring and fighting terrorism. Is it wise or effective for us to attack a country that might want to attack us before it gets the chance to? Or do such preemptive measures increase the likelihood of terrorism in the future by giving terrorists an excuse to hate us? These are the questions you must answer to determine how you feel about the war on terror, and they are questions that only time can ultimately answer.

Three Questions to Consider

1 In your opinion, do you think 9/11 has been used by politicians as a political weapon?

2 Do you think war is an effective way of dealing with terrorism? If not, do you see a better way?

3 Do you believe personal rights should ever be compromised in the interest of national security?

War

War is a reality of modern life. In many countries, the daily violence of war has become the ordinary experience of civilians. For most of its history, America has been fortunate; although we've been involved in many wars and international conflicts, our geographical distance from any powerful enemies has enabled us to distance ourselves from the reality of war. September 11 made that no longer possible. Today war for Americans is no longer a philosophical question; it is a reality we have to deal with.

And there is no question that is more politically dividing than the question of war. When, if ever, is it right to go to war? Who are the real enemies? How should we go to war, and who can we trust as allies?

From a theological perspective, the question of war has a long and confusing history. All evidence indicates that the early church was undivided in its adherence to pacifism. Although a handful of early Christians probably served as soldiers, many others quit that occupation after converting to Christianity, and Christian citizens and philosophers were often accused of supporting chaos and anarchy because of their unwillingness to support the Roman ideals of war.

The Christian perspective on war began to change in the fourth and fifth centuries when Saint Augustine wrote *City of God* and proposed his "just war" theory. Augustine's ideas, later expanded by Thomas Aquinas, have become an international philosophical standard in determining when and how nations are justified in going to war.

Augustine's criteria for determining whether a proposed war is just can be summarized by six principles:

 The war must have a just cause [self-defense or a response to clear aggression].

The war must be lawfully declared by a lawful authority [in other words, a recognized government that has the power to declare war].

 The war should be motivated by good intentions.

 War should be a last resort and should be used only after all peaceful means have been exhausted.

 The war should have a reasonable chance of success.

 The goal of the war should be to reestablish peace.

There are also four principles guiding the methods by which a just war should be waged:

 Noncombatants and civilians should never be harmed in war.

 A war should make use only of appropriate and proportional force.

The winner of a war should show respect and mercy for the defeated.

 Individual soldiers in a war should follow international agreements for conventions of war.

At first glance, it seems it would be easy to evaluate whether a war is just by comparing the arguments for a particular war with these principles. However, in practice, history has demonstrated that it's easy for a nation to argue that any war is just. Objective evaluation of a particular war is usually much easier in hindsight.

Furthermore, leaders of nonviolence, such as Gandhi and Martin Luther King Jr., have demonstrated the power of peaceful actions, even by individuals, to change the paths of nations and governments. From that perspective, many Christians have argued against the just war theory in favor of absolute pacifism. Thomas More agreed with Augustine's criteria in theory but said that in practice, no war can ever be just. Many theologians have argued that Jesus' commands to "turn the other cheek" and "not resist evil" should be interpreted simply and literally as a command for pacifism. There are several denominations, such as the Quakers, the Mennonites, and the Amish, that have always advocated pacifism. However, most modern mainstream Christians agree with some version of the just war theory.

Choosing a Position on War

Choosing a political position on the issue of war is not a decision that can be made in a vacuum; it is a decision made in the context of a specific war. For someone who interprets Jesus' pacifist teachings as applicable to nations as well as individuals, the decision is easy. But for someone who believes there is the possibility of a just war, the issues surrounding a specific military action must be evaluated to determine whether a war is just.

The current war against terrorism has been evaluated by both sides. Those in favor of the war argue that September 11 constituted an act of aggression and that the military response to it is justified self-defense. The intention of the war on terrorism is to eliminate terror all over the world, and those who support it believe the terror is far more violent than the war being fought against it. However, those opposing the war on terror argue that such an amorphous enemy can never really be defeated, and so there is no chance of success and no way to declare victory and thus end the war. They also believe the use of force that the U.S. has demonstrated in Iraq, especially against noncombatants, has been disproportionate to the original incident. And many believe the war was begun far too early, for the purpose of vengeance, long before peaceful methods had been exhausted.

A final topic that should be considered when forming a theological opinion on the politics of war is the question of eschatology. Many mainstream denominations interpret the book of Revelation as an allegorical but historically accurate prediction of the end times. As such, it predicts  specifics of wars and conflicts that will ultimately lead to Jesus' second coming and the establishment of God's reign on earth. Christians throughout history have examined actual world events in hopes of finding parallels between what's going on in the world and what's predicted in Revelation. Some Christians take the prophecies of Revelation as a responsibility for Christian nations to, for instance, support the nation of Israel in all of its military endeavors. Whether this is a reasonable position depends on your theological view.

Three Questions to Consider

1 What are your personal thoughts about war? What constitutes a just war in your opinion?

2 How did the events of September 11 affect your perspective on war?

3 Do you think the war in Iraq is a just war?

Free Versus Fair Trade

Free

Free trade. It sounds so innocent. Trade is good, right? And free—free is always good. When I first heard about free trade, I didn't have to know what it was to assume it was a good thing; the name was enough for me. But it turns out that free trade is one of the most controversial issues in the politics of foreign policy.

Truth to Know

"Here's another old saying that deserves a second look: 'Eye for eye, tooth for tooth.' Is that going to get us anywhere? Here's what I propose: 'Don't hit back at all.' If someone strikes you, stand there and take it. If someone drags you into court and sues for the shirt off your back, giftwrap your best coat and make a present of it. And if someone takes unfair advantage of you, use the occasion to practice the servant life. No more tit-for-tat stuff. Live generously.

"You're familiar with the old written law, 'Love your friend,' and its unwritten companion, 'Hate your enemy.' I'm challenging that. I'm telling you to love your enemies. Let them bring out the best in you, not the worst. When someone gives you a hard time, respond with the energies of prayer, for then you are working out of your true selves, your God-created selves. This is what God does. He gives his best — the sun to warm and the rain to nourish — to everyone, regardless: the good and bad, the nice and nasty."

(Matthew 5:38-45)

The opposite of free trade in the world of politics is not expensive trade, though it sounds like it ought to be, but fair trade. You might have heard of fair-trade coffee, which has something to do with highly caffeinated hippies who refuse to drink Starbucks because it's "the man." The problem with free trade, according to its opponents, is that the globalization of a market encourages corporations to find the lowest possible manufacturing costs and the highest paying possible market. For example, if there's no tariff to transport goods across the U.S.–Mexico border, then a steel company could manufacture products in Mexico, where labor is cheaper, and then sell the products in the U.S. This is good for the company, but it might not always be good for the laborers or for the environment because both labor laws and environmental regulations are a lot less strict in Mexico. [In 1994, the North American Free Trade Agreement (NAFTA) created a free-trade zone among the U.S., Canada, and Mexico. Since then, no tariffs or taxes have been imposed on the transfer of goods across the borders of those three countries.]

The biggest international supporter of free trade is the World Trade Organization (WTO). There are about 150 countries that are members of the WTO, all of whom impose only minimal tariffs on imports from other member countries. The goal of the WTO is basically to promote free trade by lowering trade barriers and helping countries negotiate trade agreements. However, the WTO has been criticized pretty much since its inception.

For one thing, the WTO is criticized for being unfairly biased in favor of big businesses. Groups like environmental organizations or worker unions are concerned that lowering tariffs enables businesses to seek out the lowest possible standards and wages. In addition to being bad for the environment and for workers, this is also bad for small businesses. Free trade often results in big businesses being able to lower prices to the point that small businesses are unable to compete. This can have far-reaching effects. For example, when NAFTA opened the U.S.–Mexico border, U.S. factory farms, supported by U.S. government subsidies, began selling corn in Mexico at a price that was lower than the actual cost of growing corn. Hundreds of small farms in Mexico were driven out of business, unable to

sustain their farms with such a low market price for their commodity. As a result, many of those farmers turned to different crops that would bring in better cash—like marijuana.

Free trade is a great demonstration of the limitations of a capitalist market economy. It's the Darwinist market: survival of the fittest. In free trade, businesses are encouraged to lower their prices by whatever means. It's great for big businesses that can afford to seek out the lower-cost opportunities, and it's great for the consumer who wants the lowest-priced product. However, the costs are paid in other ways, often in areas that are completely unrelated to the original product.

Fair

Fair trade, on the other hand, places a limit on the market. It's a limited form of capitalism that doesn't allow businesses to take advantage of everything they can. The international certification standard for fair-trade products has several criteria. Fair-trade companies must pay a fair wage to their employees, they must use environmentally sustainable practices, they must be open to public accountability, they must provide healthy working conditions, and they must provide assistance to producers if possible. In many cases, companies are required to pay a certain price to the producers, no matter what the market value of the product is. For example, fair-trade coffee can never be bought for less than a certain price — a price that guarantees a fair living wage to the small coffee farmer. That way, no matter how low the market price of coffee goes, fair-trade farmers can always make a living selling coffee.

Fair trade is not just a market strategy; it is a means of reducing poverty worldwide, especially in developing countries. By insisting that businesses pay wages that can support workers and that consumers pay prices that enable businesses to thrive, rather than paying a fluctuating market price, fair trade enables developing countries to become players in the world market. However, opponents criticize its insistence on intervening in the market system. Fair trade does not allow prices to be determined by market value, supply, and demand. Since it determines prices based on living wages rather than market demand, opponents argue that it is really just another form of subsidy, an artificial kind of protectionism that only increases the dependency of the developing country. Because it's motivated by political considerations rather than economic ones, they believe it's not a sustainable strategy in the world economy.

Basically, the question of free versus fair trade comes down to how much one believes in the power of the capitalist market. Should prices be completely determined by supply and demand, or should they also be influenced by political or ethical concerns? Should the world economy be a Darwinian jungle where the fittest survive and those who can't compete are left to starve and become extinct? Is it okay for the big department stores of the world to drive all the family-owned corner stores out of business? And are you personally willing to pay $4.50 for a cup of fair-trade coffee when you could get a regular cup for $1.25 in the shop around the corner? [*I think that gives us all a few questions to think about!*]

Three Questions to Consider

1 Do you think the WTO is a good organization? Why or why not?

2 Has free trade had a positive effect on our economy? If so, at what expense?

3 If you believe in fair trade, would you be willing to personally sacrifice time and money so that others have fair wages?

Immigration

A 2002 poll by Zogby International indicated a surprising difference in opinion on border issues from those on different sides of the U.S.–Mexican border. According to the poll, 58 percent of Mexicans agreed that "the territory of the United States' Southwest rightfully belongs to Mexico."[17]

Well, that might explain all the border crossings, huh?

Part of Our History

Immigration has been a political issue in the U.S. for longer than the country has existed. Back when the Pilgrims first came to the New World, Native American chiefs debated whether or not to allow the immigration or to drive the people out. And ever since then, America has become home to a myriad of immigrants and foreigners who waste no time in settling in and making themselves at home.

Exactly to what extent immigrants make themselves at home here is usually what determines how resistant the existing population is to them. Immigrants who fit in are generally welcomed by everyone; it's when immigrants try to preserve some of their own language and culture that they become a political issue. Most Americans didn't mind the cheap labor of immigrant workers until Hispanics became so prevalent that Americans had to be able to speak Spanish to find their way around downtown in major cities of the South and Southwest. Sections of New York like Little Cuba and Little Italy are quaint and attractive until they start spreading all over the city. It's often not the number of immigrants total but the number of immigrants who don't speak English that bothers people.

But hey, aren't we the melting pot?
However, many Americans are also well aware of the benefits of immigration. If nothing else, we have to remember that we all started out, however far back in our family tree, as immigrants. The Americas are different from any European country in our tradition of immigration; we are, after all, the New World, and as such we are populated by a new people. The

British, the Germans, the Spanish, and the French all have among their own nations a commonality of race, culture, language, history, and literature to unite them as people of one nationality. But in America, nationality feels much more like a hit-or-miss accident of birth and location than an overriding and definite cultural identity. Being French is a way of life; being American can encompass anything a person wants to include in the equation.

The Political Ideas

Various actions have been proposed by different political groups in an effort to influence the issues surrounding immigration. The most extreme response is, of course, to crack down on all illegal immigration and either decrease or cut off completely the number of legal immigrants allowed every year. Unlike most political issues, the biggest obstacle to this method is not a political one but a physical one: the mere physical impossibility of truly controlling a border as large as the U.S.'s. Effectively patrolling just the U.S.–Mexican border would require more people than we have in the entire army; doing it with the border guard—even with the addition of the National Guard, as has been proposed—is like trying to stop the tide with your bare hands. There's simply way too much distance to physically prevent everyone from coming in. Even a fence all along the border, besides being incredibly expensive, would not be a foolproof barrier. And that's not even considering the Canadian border.

The most extreme option on the other side of the scale is to offer amnesty to existing aliens. This basically solves the problem of illegal immigrants not by getting rid of immigrants but by making them no longer illegal. Let everyone stay and then figure out how we can all live together as a happy family.

Between these two extremes are as many different solutions as there are politicians. Some support the creation of a work-visa program that would enable immigrants to enter easily for the purpose of working in the U.S. Some support an easier path to citizenship for immigrants, especially for those who are already in the country, even if their method of entering was illegal.

There are two groups of people whose interests must be balanced when considering the problems of immigration. First, there are the immigrants. Entering a new country is a difficult and challenging prospect. Immigrants must learn a new language, navigate their way through a new culture, and respect laws they might not even know exist. Although some American citizens are unsympathetic to the challenges of immigrant life, the truth is that all Americans are, at least to some extent, immigrants themselves. If we are going to prevent immigrants from entering, we must have a good reason for doing so.

This brings me to the second group whose interests must be considered: the American citizens who are already here. For many of us, the volume and speed of immigration has reached an alarming rate in recent years. The fear of terrorism has exacerbated our fear of strangers and aliens. The presence of other cultures and languages has come to be seen not as an asset but as a threat to the American way of life. For many, the immigration issue in America is of great concern.

Three Questions to Consider

1 Should America still be considered the melting pot?

2 What are your thoughts about amnesty for immigrants?

3 How would having a dual-language country help or hurt us?

The Issues That Affect Our Future

Education

If you think about it, it's a little strange that education is a political issue. On the one hand, education is a personal issue — it's your own choice whether you want to learn or not. And on the other hand, it's a family issue—your parents probably have some say in whether or not you go to college, and they may front most of the cost. But maybe it does make sense that education is a topic of great political debate. If, as the proverb says, it takes a village to raise a child, then surely it's appropriate for society as a whole—in other words, politics—to take an interest in how well it's succeeding at educating its children.

Just add money?

There are various methods to improve American education that have been proposed in recent years. One of the most popular methods on both sides of the political spectrum, but especially on the liberal side, is to throw more money at the system. This method is considered especially effective in helping really bad school districts, which are usually either very urban or very rural. Since those districts tend to have less money than higher-performing districts, politicians figure that giving them more money is bound to help them. However, statistics show that it doesn't really help that much. Up to a point, it is helpful for a district to have more money [for example, if a school has to limit the number of copies

 a teacher can make during the school year, that tends to really cut down on the number of worksheets and tests a teacher can give out—not that that's necessarily

a bad thing]. And, of course, teacher salaries can make a difference in the quality of education because better teachers will want to make more money. However, indiscriminately adding money to a system that isn't working doesn't necessarily make the system any better.

More tests?

Despite the fact that most of us *hate* tests, another method that's been adopted in recent years at both the state and federal levels is the institution of standardized tests. In the past ten years, standardized tests have become more and more important for education, so much so that now schools can actually be closed down if their students don't meet the minimum performance requirements of the tests. This method is especially favored by conservatives, who tend to believe that everyone should conform and therefore really like the conformity [note the similarity in the words] of a standardized test. However, there are hundreds of objections to these tests, including the argument that teachers end up "teaching to the test" by training students to answer multiple-choice questions correctly rather than teaching them to think. Whether this method will really create a more successful American school system still remains to be seen.

School vouchers?!?

A third method that is even more popular with conservatives is school vouchers. This is another version of the liberal throw-money-at-the-school-system method, except it's a lot more selective. With school vouchers, parents are given a tax credit based on how many school-age children they have. They then get to put the tax credit toward any school they choose, including private or religious schools. This method has faced a lot of opposition, partly from people who are worried about federal tax money going to religious schools and partly from people who are worried about bad schools [the ones that really need the money] losing all their students and therefore all their money. The beneficial side of this idea is that it brings the methods of capitalism into education by creating a competitive system. The best schools prosper, and the bad schools go under, just like good and bad businesses. The problem, of course, is that there's a good chance some students would end up left behind at the bad schools if for some reason [transportation being the main one] they weren't able, despite the tax money, to get to a better school. However, because of these controversies this idea hasn't been adopted, so there's no telling how well it would work.

Other Options

A final education method that has become very popular, especially in high-quality school systems, is the magnet school.

Magnet schools focus their studies on a particular academic [or even extracurricular] area. Some are technological; some emphasize creative or liberal arts; some provide bilingual education from an early grade. These schools are very popular with students and parents alike. Their disadvantage is mostly the fact that usually only the best school systems have the resources to implement them. Also, they add a lot more options for the best students, but they don't do much for students who are falling behind.

It's easy for politicians to say that improving education is an important item on their platform. But before you believe them, investigate which programs they want to implement and not just what they say they want to accomplish. They might want to reward good teachers with bonuses and incentives, which is a more directed use of money, but it could lead [shocking as it is] to teachers cheating by giving good grades to students who don't deserve them. Or they might want to threaten the staff of bad schools with firings and renovation, using negative instead of positive incentives to scare teachers and administrators into teaching better. Before you vote, decide for yourself what method you think will help the most.

Three Questions to Consider

1 Should education even be a political issue? Why or why not?

2 Do you think standardized testing is an effective way of measuring competency?

3 Are school vouchers fair to students from low-income families?

Energy — The Little Problem That Could . . .

[well, who knows?]

How energy is used, conserved, and developed has only recently become an issue in major political platforms. Environmentalists, of course, have kept energy at the forefront of debate for years, but most voters have not considered it a core issue. However, recent events such as Hurricane Katrina and steadily rising gas prices have made this issue one that touches voters' wallets and therefore their ballots. [*You don't mess with Americans' wallets — at least not without a fight, vote, or hissy fit!*]

Ironically, in the energy debate it is the liberal party that tends to be on the side of conservation. Republicans are traditionally conservative, but in this case, conservative means not conservation but preservation of the status quo. The status quo in the energy debate means the preservation of a lifestyle that has developed in an age of unprecedented cheap energy.

What's the big deal?

Well, in simple terms it's the old adage called supply and demand. For years cheap, easily available energy — mostly in the form of petrochemicals — has led to a lifestyle of specialization and abundance. Think about it:

- ⊕ Food can be grown in monoculture farms, shipped to factories on the other side of the country for processing, and then shipped to yet another corner of the country to be sold, all because it's cheaper to transport the food than to grow, process, and eat it all in the same place.

- ⊕ Average Americans live anywhere from ten to fifty miles from work and travel that distance twice daily in a car by themselves, allowing them to enjoy both the safety of the suburbs and the job bank of the city using the convenience of personal transportation, all because it's cheaper to commute than to live in the city.

- ⊕ A successful business can quickly develop into a national chain due to the ease of communication and transportation over great distances.

In other words, the American lifestyle — *the American dream* — has been formed by, and is utterly dependent on, cheap energy.

However, some believe there are clear warning signs that this energy age is swiftly coming to an end. Major politicians and economists, such as Matt Simmons and Al Gore, have begun to warn of a coming energy collapse in the form of peak oil. And there is increasing public resistance to dependence on a volatile Middle East for our primary source of energy. More and more policy makers are lobbying for alternative forms of energy such as ethanol, wind, and solar and nuclear energy.

Though political answers are few, here are the core problems. Two core issues drive the energy debate. The first and most recent is the unreliability of energy supply due to political instability in source countries [Venezuela and Saudi Arabia are the U.S.'s main suppliers of oil] and the current production plateau that could be a warning sign of the peaking of world oil. The second and most long-standing is pollution — in our cities, in our waterways, and in the heartland.

Many politicians [on both sides of the aisle] agree that energy supply is and will continue to be an issue in American politics. For more information, read *The Party's Over: Oil, War and the Fate of Industrial Societies* by Richard Heinberg, *Twilight in the Desert: The Coming Saudi Oil Shock and the World Economy* by Matthew R. Simmons, or *Beyond Oil: The View from Hubbert's Peak* by Kenneth S. Deffeyes.

1 Why do you think the energy issue is now at the forefront of political debate? Do you think it will continue to be?

2 Do you think warnings of a pending energy collapse are legitimate?

3 Do you believe most Americans are willing to sacrifice money and convenience for better energy sources?

Environment

Environmentalism has been an important political movement since the hippie days of the seventies, reaching an even greater level when Rachel Carson's book *Silent Spring* instigated a national fear of the effects of pollution. I say important, but that's a debatable term. On the one hand, in the eleven years since the inception of the Green Party, there have been very few politicians elected to state or national positions on the Green Party platform. Not a great track record. On the other hand, environmentalists, while not very successful politicians, are darn good lobbyists; the Environmental Protection Agency gets laws passed like a little kid steals cookies from a jar. Today there are hundreds of laws on the books that were lobbied into being by the EPA.

And a lot of those laws are pretty stringent to deal with. Construction laws, for example, are particularly strict. The sighting of a single endangered animal or bird in an area can indefinitely, and many times permanently, halt all construction or development in the entire county—as countless businesses and even private landowners have discovered. And laws governing the disposal of waste have prohibited the development of countless businesses.

Nevertheless, for a long time, environmentalism was the strict concern of liberals. The stereotypical environmentalist was a hard-core hippie, complete with long hair, dirty fingernails, and Birkenstocks. However, in recent years, various movements have contributed to the adoption of environmental principles by more conservative groups. Rod Dreher's book *Crunchy Cons* outlines the growth of a strong environmental movement firmly entrenched in the Republican Party. Big business is jumping on the bandwagon with trends like General Motors' "Live Green, Go Yellow" advertisements supporting the development of ethanol-powered and flex-fuel vehicles. Al Gore's movie about global warming, *An Inconvenient Truth*, brought environmental issues before a wider audience. [Everyone goes to the movies—and even though George W. Bush said he didn't plan on seeing it, several people in his Cabinet did.]

Environmentalism is becoming more and more popular on both ends of the political spectrum. However, there are several inconsistencies on both sides.

To the left or right?

Hard-core liberal environmentalists are easy to identify. You can find them out in the woods making out with trees. Okay, so not really, but they are always united by their determination to keep nature as pristine as possible. They're in favor of laws that protect endangered species, that maintain natural wildlife areas, and that limit businesses and individuals from utilizing or exploring those areas. They are the inventors of organizations like Leave No Trace, the group that puts up the signs you might have seen at entrances to national parks: *Take nothing but pictures; leave nothing but footprints*. That's a pretty good summary of the extreme environmentalist position.

However, that isn't always possible. Scientists are realizing more and more that it's impossible for humans to "live in harmony" with nature without impacting it. This leads to a lot of revising of environmentalists' opinions. For example, at one time, the EPA was firmly against nuclear power plants. Now, thanks to the obvious problems of fossil fuels, the EPA is all about clean, renewable fuel, and nuclear power is starting to look a lot more attractive. This just goes to show that the environmentalist position has to be taken with a grain of salt because it's likely their position will change drastically whenever new scientific information comes to light. [The only thing you can really count on is that they'll always take sides with the spotted owls and the whales, even if supporting such endangered

Evangelicals Going Green? Maybe!

[and no, it's not MONEY I'm referring to]

"We affirm that God-given dominion is a sacred responsibility to steward the earth and not a license to abuse the creation of which we are a part," states the National Evangelical Association's environmental position paper titled "For the Health of the Nation." The document goes on to say, "Because clean air, pure water, and adequate resources are crucial to public health and civic order, government has an obligation to protect its citizens from the effects of environmental degradation."[18] [*But between you and me, the NAE still doesn't get it!*]

animals means taking sides against humanity, which is what opponents of environmentalism accuse them of doing.]

From the most extreme conservative perspective, it seems silly to worry about the habitat of some previously undiscovered species of worm in comparison with the lives of, say, the families of thousands of loggers whose jobs depend on destroying the worm's habitat. It's easy to demonize big business, but antienvironmentalists are quick to point out that businesses are made of people. It's easy, too, to turn the environmentalist argument against itself: If humans are part of nature, part of the ecosystem of the world, then don't we have the same responsibility that every other species demonstrates—the responsibility to propagate and expand our species as much as we can? Rabbits do it; why shouldn't we?

Ultimately, the two sides will have to find a balance between protecting the worms and protecting the humans. In the meantime, it's up to you to decide which way the scale is tipping and which way you want to push it. Lucky for you, the days are past when you need to become a Birkenstock-wearing hippie or a hard-hearted businessman to take sides on environmental issues. These days, pretty much everyone has an opinion on the environment, so please don't be an exception.

Wanna go Green? Check out the Green Party website at www.gp.org. Or for more information about environmental issues, visit the EPA's website at www.epa.gov.

Three Questions to Consider

1 Why do you think the environment has become a central concern to both the Republican and Democratic Parties?

2 To what extent do you think development should be compromised to preserve the environment?

3 Do you believe that Christians, as stewards of God's creation, have a responsibility to preserve the environment?

Taxes

[wouldn't it suck to work for the IRS on April 15?]

Everyone knows the two things that are certain in life: death and taxes. [*Well, that and also that you'll get annoyed with Jerry Falwell at least once in your lifetime.*] However, you may not know that taxes, like taxpayers, are not always created equal.

[*You totally knew that, huh?*]

For most Americans, the proverb is pretty true, and taxes are a lot like death: something you can't really avoid but you just have to put up with. Naturally, everyone who pays taxes—which is everyone, unless, of course, a person evades them—wants to pay less. So every politician claims that his or her goal is to lower taxes. But of course when evaluating a political candidate on his or her tax position, it's always wise to remember that all politicians are paid by tax dollars, so any candidate's proposal for lowering taxes is suspect.

However, candidates are also well aware that lowering taxes is the most attractive thing they can do for their political appeal. [*And they want to be liked*—their income is also dependent on getting elected and staying in office, right?]

All politicians *say* they want to lower taxes as part of their platform, but, um, the Dems and the Repubs emphasize different things.

The D Side
The Democratic Party tends to emphasize the need to lower taxes for middle- and lower-income families, as opposed to the wealthy. This is generally an effective argument, since hardly anyone really thinks of themselves as wealthy, and political

candidates don't have to get into details [like, for example, they could be referring to anyone who makes more than $40,000 a year as wealthy, and no one would ever know]. Any argument about the politics of taxes is usually dependent on the fact that no one outside of the IRS really understands taxes [and not many people inside the IRS, either]. So the Democrats can claim to have a plan that will lower taxes for everyone except the wealthy without having to define who is wealthy or how the plan will work.

The R Side

Republicans might even be a little worse. They also claim to support plans that will lower taxes for everyone, especially lower-income families, but they couch the plans in terms that are confusing at best. They are especially concerned about the "marriage penalty," the current "tax brackets," and the "death tax" [which I assume has something to do with the proverbial connection between death and taxes]. Voters who support programs that repeal or lower these dreaded taxes tend to smile and nod knowingly when these topics come up, without actually understanding anything about what they mean.

Both parties, of course, are taking advantage of the fact that the current tax code is some sixty thousand pages long and requires multiple degrees just to understand it. It is estimated that Americans collectively spend $125 billion a year consulting experts and studying the system just to comply with the tax code—and then we still have to pay the taxes.

As a result, there are several grassroots movements pushing for income tax reform. The two biggest movements at present are the flat tax and the fair tax. Proponents of both argue that the income tax has become too complicated and too specialized to be either realistic or fair. They argue that the income tax not only shows far too much favoritism to various special interest groups but also is so difficult to follow that the government loses an estimated $200 billion a year due to noncompliance—much of which is inadvertent due to taxpayers' misunderstandings of the tax code laws.

Flat Tax

Both the flat tax and the fair tax call for a complete reform of the income tax system. The flat tax is exactly what it sounds like: It calls for a single, flat rate of income tax on all taxpayers. Every family would receive deductions for living expenses based on the number of people in the family [a family of four would receive four deductions], but after that, the family income would be taxed at a single, flat rate that's the same for everyone across the board. This method is obviously a lot simpler than our current system.

Fair Tax

The fair tax calls for an even bigger change: It argues for a repeal of the income tax entirely. Income tax was illegal in the U.S. until 1913 when the Sixteenth Amendment legalized it. The fair tax calls for a return to the days before income tax and for federal funding to come from a retail sales tax that would be included by businesses in the price of all goods and services. The advantage of this system is that it would completely dispense with the bureaucracy of the income tax: The IRS would be obsolete, and April 15 would be just another day. Individuals would no longer be required to report income at all. Like the flat tax, the fair tax would give a rebate [or rather a prebate] to all families based on the taxes they would pay on their income up to the poverty level, so their basic living expenses would not be taxed. All expenses after that would be taxed by a simple sales tax — again, the same rate for everyone. But since the rich generally spend a lot more discretionary income than the poor, the fair tax would end up taxing the rich more than the poor, just without the red tape to prove it.

Three Questions to Consider

1 Does your perspective on taxes align more with the Democratic or Republican Party?

2 Do you believe wealthy people should have to pay a higher percentage of taxes?

3 Does either the flat tax or the fair tax seem like an effective way to reform our tax system?

How *You* Get Involved

[if there was a *u* in politics, this section would be it]

Politics, it seems to me, for years, or all too long, has been concerned with right or left instead of right or wrong.

— Richard Armour

You're going to love this section! Why? Because it's about you. You're excited, huh? You probably never expected to be the topic of one of my books. But hey, we've spent an awful lot of time together over the last two hundred pages or so, and the people I hang with usually end up in a book at some point. Being included in a book should be considered an honor, unless of course it tells a secret you don't want released to the public.

And for some of you, there are secrets to share.

But don't worry, I'm not going to be sharing anything personal. I'm not planning on outing any politically liberal Christian college students—your secret is safe with me. [*And, yes, there are more Christians who are politically liberal and spiritually conservative than you may think.*] We certainly wouldn't want *that* to get around campus, now would we? [*Believe me, I understand.*] And those of you who have been raised in liberal, open-minded churches [*and voted for W*], your secret is safe also. I'm an equal-opportunity Christian writer. [*I just want us all to get along!*]

AND POLITICS ARE PERSONAL BUSINESS.

But the "it's personal" aspect is one of the many great things about politics [*other great things include presidential scandals, first-lady hairstyles, and Diane Sawyer!*]. Seriously, politics is a personal choice that *you* get to make. But like most serious things where the ultimate choice is up to you, there's also a lot of responsibility that comes with making political decisions. So allow me the grace to be a wee bit inspirational for a moment: Your political decisions shouldn't be taken lightly. As Christians, I believe we should be involved in the political process. But politics can get ugly. All of us have seen the mean-spiritedness of those "debates" on the Congressional floor. However, that doesn't mean we have to stoop to the same level. As followers of Jesus, we should handle this political responsibility with integrity, wisdom, and humility, not with cockiness and control.

Unfortunately, when Christianity and politics become married to one another, it's often an ugly union. And it's often a rather forced marriage at times. Let's face it: Some Christians wonder if it's a union that's supposed to exist in the first place, due to the separation of church and state. But there's a big difference between letting your faith affect your politics and trying to marry the two. In other words, involvement, support, and influence don't always have to imply partnership [and certainly not a manipulative partnership].

Sadly, however, the world of politics often brings out the worst in people [*kind of like the Academy Awards brings out the worst in a star's fashion!*]. If you watch or read anything about the antics in Washington DC, you know that politics can get ugly. And to some extent, we shouldn't expect much more, really. I mean, politics is little more than a bunch of humans trying to manage the state of the nation. And whenever you give that kind of power, influence, and control to a whole bunch of humans who are often trying to change the status quo, there are going to be times when it gets as ugly as senior citizens in bikinis. But just because it's ugly *doesn't* mean Christians should avoid the process.

In fact, you should *engage* the process. This section focuses on the ways you can be involved in politics!

Let's get it on . . . or at least get started.

Ways You Can Be Involved

Register to vote.
[you'd be surprised how many don't register]

This might seem rather simple, but voting is the first and foremost way for you to be involved. Not voting says you don't care. Not voting implies apathy. And between you and me,

You can't put in your two cents about who should be our president until you have done the legwork. Here are a few places you can get that done now.

RocktheVote.org. Touting itself as "political power for young people," this site enables users to register to vote, update their address, change parties, read the Rock the Vote blog, and even become the site's friend on MySpace. Users can also become politically active by joining street teams and encouraging others to "rock the vote." In the last major election, Rock the Vote registered 1.4 million people.

DeclareYourself.org. Similar to Rock the Vote, Declare Yourself is dedicated to mobilizing young Americans to register and vote.

GoVote.org. Considerably less cool than Rock the Vote, Go Vote serves the same basic purpose. Users can register to vote in "four easy steps," send text messages to family and friends to get them to vote, and sign up to volunteer in their local community. While the site doesn't offer a lot of extras, it does accomplish its purpose of registering people to vote.

Congress.org. A more robust site than the sites specifically geared for registering, Congress.org offers a wealth of information for American citizens. In addition to registering to vote, users can write to their elected officials, post comments about issues, and a lot more.

The library, post office, or local election office. These places usually have all the paperwork needed to register.

So go register to vote! And don't do it because Daddy told you to; do it because it's the right thing to do.

I'd rather see someone vote for the candidate I dislike than sit back and be apathetic about the process. If you're eighteen or older, there's *no* reason you should not be registered. Registering is the first step toward making a difference.

Choose a party affiliation.

[Democrat, Republican, independent, or any of the other choices]

When you register to vote, you'll be asked to either affiliate yourself with a political party or to register as an independent. We've talked about the Democratic Party versus the Republican Party quite a bit in this book, but when you sign up to vote, it will be time to truly consider if you want to align yourself with one of the parties *or* if you want politicians to have to work extra hard for your vote. Well, to help you make this decision, we've put together a comparison chart to give you a quick reference guide to the stereotypical differences between elephants and donkeys. [*It's a very complicated decision: Do you want to be fat? Or do you want to be an ass?*]

Facts About the Elephants

The Republican Party started in the early 1850s in Wisconsin, of all places [*which today is, um, NOT known for its Republicanness*]. The slogan of their first presidential campaign was "Free soil, free labor, free speech, free men, Fremont," which was for candidate John C. Fremont. It wasn't until the following presidential election that Abe Lincoln became the first Republican president.[1] Some well-known Republican presidents include Richard Nixon, Theodore Roosevelt, Dwight Eisenhower, Ronald Reagan, and the Bushes. Now, you might also be wondering, *Where did the elephant come from?* Well, it came from nineteenth-century cartoonist Thomas Nast; it was part of a political cartoon that appeared in *Harper's Weekly*.[2] Though the party once stood for antislavery and labor, today things have changed. With a little help from the elephant, I present the BIG points of the Republican platform.

Big ears help them hear God! A good number of Republicans are churchgoing Caucasians who want prayer in schools.

Wherever this fellow sits, it becomes his environment; he doesn't care about what plants he smashes. The rule is this: Environment after economy except right before elections.

Everybody needs a big gun in the house. Gun control is for wimps.

A big mouth helps Republicans chew up the Democrats' higher-tax laws and spit them out. Taxes are for Democrats!

Big feet help the Republicans stomp all over the pro-choicers in a mass stampede! Abortion is frowned upon.

Size matters to Republicans, especially when it comes to business, military, and America's Christian heritage.

Facts About the Donkeys

The Democratic Party was begun by Thomas Jefferson in the late 1700s. According to Ron Brown, former chairman of the Democratic Party, they are the party—from Jefferson to Bill Clinton—that has stood behind "an abiding faith in the judgment of hardworking American families, and a commitment to helping the excluded, the disenfranchised and the poor strengthen our nation by earning themselves a piece of the American Dream."[3] Of course, Democrats fail to mention they were also the party that once stood behind slavery. Famous Democratic presidents include Jefferson, Clinton, Franklin D. Roosevelt, John F. Kennedy, and Jimmy Carter. The history of the Democratic donkey dates back to Andrew Jackson; his opponents called him a jackass, so he used the image on his campaign signs. Thomas Nast, the same artist who drew the elephant, drew the donkey.[4] The Democratic Party has changed over the years and today builds its platform on the following ideals.

Though the donkey is small, Democrats are big when it comes to the minimum wage, rights for gays and lesbians, and gun control!

These big ears help the Democrats listen to Americans who support the right of women to choose what they can and cannot do with their bodies. The Democratic platform is pro-abortion.

These feet may be small, but they are perfect for trekking the uphill battle toward protecting America's flag burners, tree huggers, and those pesky poor people the Republicans deny are out there.

These eyes help the Dems see what the "fiscally conservative" Republicans have done to America's budget, and they don't like it one bit.

Still not sure which party you want to join? Well, here are three interviews with Christians—a Democrat, a Republican, and an independent—in which they explain why they chose their party affiliation.

Ten Questions with a Christian Independent

Sharon Kuykendall shares how her faith helps her decide her politics.

MPT: Tell us a little about your background.

SHARON: I grew up in California, Hawaii, and Maryland. We were a Christian—and VERY Republican—family; in fact, my mom was born in China to missionary parents. I went to church-run schools from first grade through college, where I got a BA in history with minors in secondary education and communications. It was Christian everything, even summer camp!

MPT: Why do you personally believe politics are important?

SHARON: Because as imperfect as the system is—and always will be, since it's constructed by humans—it's what we have and what shapes the world we live in and the values that determine how we treat the rest of the world.

MPT: Describe your theology in five words.

SHARON: Honesty. Mercy. Justice. Accountability. Grace.

MPT: What American politician [past or present] do you most identify with?

SHARON: I can't think of any one person I've agreed with completely, but I think Benjamin Franklin had a unique ability to see both the good and bad of human nature and how it will always form politics.

MPT: How does faith influence your political opinions?

SHARON: No person, government, or country will ever be perfect, but as much as possible I want my votes and my tax dollars to maintain policies that bring out the best attributes of human nature that God has given us and that treat people as God would want them to be treated. This is less about forcing my views on everyone else and more about helping my country be what I hope we can be.

MPT: How do you choose who to vote for?

SHARON: I try to have an educated opinion about the issues and then see which candidates have platforms that are *closest* to what I believe and are honest, earnest, and capable of following through. I've learned that just because a candidate holds a position I agree with — pro-life, for example — that doesn't mean he or she will be the most effective in that position. Some politicians are so dogmatic they end up hurting their most cherished causes.

MPT: What are the three biggest influences that helped you form your current political opinions?

SHARON: My grandfather was very active in the California Republican Party his entire adult life — I have the letters and Christmas cards from Nixon to prove it! My mother encouraged me from an early age to be curious and to read, read, read everything I could about all issues. And finally, current affairs and history: Where we've been has to teach us something about where we're headed.

MPT: If you could change one thing in the current American political scene, what would it be?

SHARON: That people would listen to opposing viewpoints — it strengthens what we believe and shows us angles we may not have thought about. And that we would stop labeling people as unpatriotic or unAmerican just because they have different political opinions than we do. Fighting for free speech and thought is rather hollow when it's not tolerated among ourselves.

MPT: What is the best thing the church is doing politically right now? What is the worst thing?

SHARON: I don't believe there is one specific church we can attribute things to. But I appreciate members of the Christian community who are showing compassion and support to soldiers, fellow citizens, and those suffering around the world, regardless of the country. The worst thing is the dogmatic "we have the only RIGHT answers and you are unAmerican if you disagree with us" mentality of so many church groups.

MPT: In your opinion, what's the most important issue in America's politics today?

SHARON: The shift from sharing the story of God's grace and the gift of his Son to attempting to legislate morality through the court system. We need to get back to the real reason for being here. I've been struck lately by a quote from John Paul II: "Freedom exists not to do what you like but to have the right to do what you ought."

Ten Questions with a Christian Republican

Rich Shipe talks about his personal love of conservative politics.

MPT: Tell us a little about your background.

RICH: I spent my childhood in Denver, Colorado, and my teen years to the present in northern Virginia right at the edge of urban sprawl about forty-five miles west of DC. A big thing that defined me was that my parents were crazy enough to try homeschooling me at a time when no one knew what homeschooling was. I went to Grove City College but dropped out to work on a couple of political campaigns. One thing led to another, and I've never gone back to finish my degree. I am the world's definition of uneducated.

MPT: Why do you personally believe politics are important?

RICH: It is very important if you live in a democracy. "We the People . . ." is how our Constitution starts, and it means that the people, organized into a democratic republic, are the highest authority. If you don't agree that this is important, then you should move to North Korea, where they have a dictatorship and the only person who matters is Kim Jong-il. This isn't to imply that government is the most important thing, but at least cast thoughtful votes each election!

MPT: What American politician [past or present] do you most identify with?

RICH: Probably Reagan because he was such a strong communicator and held deep convictions on the value of human life. He was the only president to publish a book while in office, a little hardcover book called *Abortion and the Conscience of the Nation*. There are very few politicians today who have that kind of guts. I don't identify with that kind of courage, but I certainly admire it.

MPT: Describe your theology in five words.

RICH: Christian. It means what it means. I don't need to qualify or modify it.

MPT: How does faith influence your political opinions?

RICH: Faith influences all of my life. That is a huge question, and I could fill a full book with the answer — and many others have. I start with Micah 6:8, which says,

> He has told you, O man, what is good;
> And what does the Lord require of you
> But to do justice, to love kindness,
> And to walk humbly with your God? (NASB)

Too often our government does injustice and attacks kindness, and our leaders constantly walk in pride.

MPT: How do you choose who to vote for?

RICH: It is hard, but I always try to vote for the person who is closest to my views on the issues yet has a realistic chance of winning. There is a time for long-shot third party candidates, but we've got to think long-term and be strategic in our approach.

MPT: What are the three biggest influences that helped you form your current political opinions?

RICH: (a) the Bible, (b) Francis Schaeffer's book *A Christian Manifesto*, and (c) probably the hundreds of influences from friends, family, speeches, articles, and related books.

MPT: If you could change one thing in the current American political scene, what would it be?

RICH: From a spiritual standpoint, it would be national revival. That would change the political scene because we, the people, would be changed. From a political standpoint, I think the biggest thing we've lost since our founding is the federalist system of government. It was such a genius idea to divide the government up into federal, state, and local. Centralized government sucks, and local government rocks.

MPT: What is the best thing the church is doing politically right now? What is the worst thing?

RICH: I struggle with that question all the time. One thing I know is that our brothers and sisters in Christ often make mistakes. I'm not really sure what we are doing right, but I do know we aren't loving enough. We've got to see the world through the eyes of Christ. Clearly the church struggles with its role, and that role is particularly tough in a democracy of "We the People." From a political standpoint, it does seem like it would be easier to live in North Korea under a dictator.

MPT: In your opinion, what's the most important issue in America's politics today?

RICH: Probably all the issues related to the value of life. Our nation has struggled with abortion and is beginning to struggle with other aspects of the right to life issue, like embryonic stem cell research. Why would God allow so many babies to be killed for so long? What holds back his hand from our nation? I feel not only for the lost lives but for the mothers and fathers who struggle through them.

Ten Questions with a Christian Democrat

Carrie Ann Alford tells us why being like Jesus for her means leaning to the left.

MPT: Tell us a little about your background.

CARRIE: I grew up in a Christian home. I went to college at Moody Bible Institute, lived on campus, and spent one semester in Washington DC as an intern in the fall of 1996. I moved to DC in July of 1997 after graduation. My father claims he's an independent, but he pretty much always votes Republican. My mother is an old-school liberal Dem from the sixties.

MPT: Why do you personally believe politics are important?

CARRIE: I never knew otherwise. Both my dad's side and mom's side of the family talk about politics all the time. It was practically a contact sport on my mom's side. They were insanely supportive when I moved to DC.

MPT: Describe your theology in five words.

CARRIE: Conservative Episcopalian – high church.

MPT: What American politician [past or present] do you most identify with?

CARRIE: The one book I read as a kid – yes, I am a politics nerd – that made me fall in love with politics was Geraldine Ferraro's autobiography after the 1984 election.

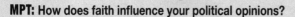

MPT: How does faith influence your political opinions?

CARRIE: My mother taught me to be like Jesus — theologically conservative, politically and socially liberal. He had unbelievable compassion for everyone, especially nonbelievers.

MPT: How do you choose who to vote for?

CARRIE: I joke around that I am a lazy voter, which is why I vote straight ticket. The truth is I truly believe in the Democratic Party and its overarching principles.

MPT: What are the three biggest influences that helped you form your current political opinions?

CARRIE: Compassion for those who don't have a voice at the political table. Righteous anger for those who can't speak up for themselves. An understanding that I chose God and that I chose to put myself under his laws, and not everyone in this country has done the same. We can't legislate morality. It hasn't worked in 2,000 years, and it never will. People have to choose good over evil (see Genesis 3).

MPT: If you could change one thing in the current American political scene, what would it be?

CARRIE: Let's all take a nap and get back to the socially polite, gracious and sophisticated, and calmer politics of the past.

MPT: What is the best thing the church is doing politically right now? What is the worst thing?

CARRIE: The best? Many churches and Christians are examining their faith, collective and personal, and asking questions about what church looks like and what we should believe. The worst? Many other Christians not only are still afraid to examine these things but also are actively out to destroy anyone who does. They say people can't be real Christians if they question things or vote certain ways. "That's a bunch of bullroar," as my father would say.

MPT: In your opinion, what's the most important issue in America's politics today?

CARRIE: I don't think there is one, except that maybe everyone, both collectively and personally, needs to be better financially. We need to save and conserve and get back to being thrifty, which was so highly prized until the 1970s. Other than that, we need to get away from "issues," in my opinion. As Rufus says in *Dogma*, "I think it's better to have ideas. You can change an idea. Changing a belief is trickier. Life should be malleable and progressive; working from idea to idea permits that. Beliefs anchor you to certain points and limit growth; new ideas can't generate. Life becomes stagnant."

Got a concern? Call your congresspeople.

One way you can be involved is by staying in contact with your congressmen and congresswomen, senators, and even the president. If you have something you want to communicate to any one of them [*you know, like you're ticked off about the gas prices*], you can! It's very easy. Most, if not all, politicians have websites that offer constituents the opportunity to communicate with them. If you don't want to go through the trouble of Googling your representative or if you don't know his or her name, visit the website for the agency in which he or she works. There you can find everything you need: mailing address, e-mail address, and phone number. Here are some sites to check:

✠ United States Senate: www.senate.gov
✠ United States House of Representatives: www.house.gov
✠ National Conference of State Legislatures: http://www .ncsl.org/public/leglinks.cfm [This site lists the websites for every state's legislature.]

Another resource is www.Congress.org. For a modest fee, it offers to print your letter and hand deliver it to Capitol Hill. You can also read what other people are writing to their political leaders on the "Read Letters to Leaders" section of the site. This resource provides a way for people to read about what issues are important to Americans nationwide.

Now, if you don't have access to the Internet, visit your local library. They can also provide you with contact information [and probably offer Internet access, too!].

If you want to write the president, his e-mail address is: president@whitehouse.gov. His mailing address is:

The White House
1600 Pennsylvania Avenue NW
Washington, DC 20500

The vice president's e-mail address is: vice.president@whitehouse.gov.

When writing to the president or other members of office, keep these helpful hints in mind:

- Be concise: Politicians are busy people and will appreciate your brevity.
- Be legible: Typing is best, but if you choose to handwrite your letter, make sure it is neat and easy to read.
- Be factual: Using facts and your personal story can help strengthen your letter and support your cause.

The White House also offers interactive chats on "Ask the White House" (http://www.whitehouse.gov/ask/). Since launching this resource in April 2003, the White House has

If you must . . .	Never . . .	Instead, try . . .	And you'll be . . .
Put political bumper stickers on your car . . .	Mix your Christianity with your political message. Nobody cares that you actually think God told you to vote for [fill in the blank]!	Keeping your message simple. [Fill in the blank] for president 2012!	Letting people know how you feel without letting them know too much about how you feel. Remember, sometimes mystery is a very good thing. [And not letting the world know that you think God is a Republican is a good kind of mystery!]

TOGETHER WE STAND . . .

hosted more than two hundred chats with Cabinet secretaries, senior White House officials, professionals who work behind the scenes, and others. Citizens are invited to participate in these online sessions and are able to read transcripts of past sessions.

Your options	What does it involve?	Chances of this happening?
President	Um, leading our country, silly.	One in about 300 million. But hey, every four years there's a chance.
Member of Congress	Representing a state!	Hey, Hillary did it!
Lobbyist	Representing a cause!	Pretty good. Even better if you actually have a cause you halfway believe in.
News reporter	Delivering your version of the truth on TV, the Internet, and anywhere else they'll let you voice it.	You being Katie Couric? Eh, not too good.
Activist	Holding up signs and getting mildly violent when necessary.	AWESOME! Just make a sign.
White House intern	Um, do we have to go there?	I guess that depends on what you're willing to do to get there. . . . Only the best make it in!
Radio talk-show host	Voicing your opinion to everyone who is listening.	Um, Rush Limbaugh does it; I think you can, too.
Volunteer	Doing whatever a political party needs you to do.	Just make a phone call!
Sign person	Sticking political signs in the ground in key locations around a community.	Get a hammer and a few nails, and you have yourself a job.

Your options	Best privileges?	Hey, it beats ...	Should you do it?
President	Choosing the colors of some White House rugs. Getting to make love in the Oval Office to the first lady or first man.	Flipping burgers.	As long as you know that everything you do will be written into history. And people will be studying your actions for a very long time.
Member of Congress	Impeachment privileges.	Studying for an economics final.	NO! Ha ha! Just kidding. You should totally go for it!
Lobbyist	Getting influential people tipsy [accidentally, of course!].	Being Lynne Cheney's third cousin. Relating without benefits stinks!	I think so. Just be honest with yourself. Lobbying can be awfully difficult.
News reporter	Delivering your version of the truth on TV, the Internet, and anywhere else they'll let you voice it.	Working for the government.	Yep, writing and being on TV is fun.
Activist	Making up the clever slogan for your sign.	Holding up signs for a car wash fundraiser.	If you believe in a cause, I think you should!
White House intern	"Coffee, Mr. President?"	Well, you'll have to let us know what it beats.	Only if you have stamina; walking from your desk to the coffee machine could be hard on your tootsies.
Radio talk-show host	All the bull you get to say.	"Coffee, Mr. President?"	Is your name Ann Coulter? No? Then yes, do it.
Volunteer	Free political signs!	Having to stick those signs in the ground.	We think everyone should do it once.
Sign person	Splinters.	This job pretty much bites.	Someone has to do it.

Questions to ask	He's liberal if he says:	He's conservative if he says:	Or he might be gay if he says:
What do you want to do on Friday night?	"Well, I'd like to keep my options open. You know, just in case one of my friends comes up with a really good idea. That way, I'm not committed."	"I think I'll stay home, sit on my butt, and do nothing. I've had a really rough week."	"Your place or mine?"
If you had to choose between being dunked in a pool of vomit or covered in walrus snot, which would it be?	"Um, can I bring people with me? I mean, I think that kind of decision would require a meeting to discuss my options."	"Why can't I just shoot the guy who asked me that question? That's a dumb question, and I think the guy who came up with such a nonsensical idea should die."	"Am I naked?"
What do you think should be done about the energy crisis?	"I'm doing my part; I've been using less hot water, letting my clothes air-dry, and collecting my soda cans for recycling. I think it's something all of us can do."	"What energy crisis? There's no energy crisis. The guy who thought up that question should be shot. No, really, let me get my gun."	"I've been told that I'm energetic!"
You want me to rub that for you?	"Well, maybe. Will it hurt? Oh, darn. I don't know if you should. I'm kind of sensitive there, and it might hurt in the morning. Oh, go ahead and do it. Oh, wait!"	"Yes, but let's keep it between us, shall we?"	"Can you ask me that question again?"
How much wood could a woodchuck chuck?	"Does the woodchuck like chucking wood? Is it earning a fair wage? Any chance I could get a few more woodchucks in there to help him out?"	"Is this a Chinese woodchuck? You know those Asians are hard workers."	"I just love little woodchucks; they are so cute!"

How to Get Involved with a Political Party

[an interview with Mandy Runnels, the finance director for the Tennessee Republican Party]

Ever wanted to volunteer for a political party? Well, according to my friend Mandy Runnels, it's easier to get involved than you might think. In fact, during an election year, both sides are usually dying for a little help!

MPT: What are some ways twentysomethings can become politically involved with a party?

MANDY: Twentysomethings can call their local and state officials and/or congresspeople to offer to volunteer or intern. This might involve waving signs, stamping and sealing campaign mailings to voters, and so on for their candidate of choice during the heat of the election. If you have political connections, use them.

MPT: How much time should one be willing to donate?

MANDY: Campaigns need all the help they can get. Donate your time according to your schedule. But remember, there is no such thing as overextending yourself. The campaign is only hot for a maximum of three months.

MPT: Is it okay to volunteer even if you don't agree with everything a party stands for?

MANDY: Yes, find the party that shares the most interests with you and work for those things you believe in. You're never going to agree with the entire platform.

MPT: What do you look for in volunteers?
MANDY: Dedication, LOYALTY, and people who will devote as much time as they can and spend that time being productive. They also should realize they need to be able to take direction from someone who may be the same age as them. Organized young folks often assume volunteer coordinator positions.

Oooooh . . . and I try to make sure they are not a snitch for the other side. It happens all the time.

MPT: What's the best way for people to get in touch with their state's office for a particular party?
MANDY: Google or ask a friend who's involved. We're pretty open to walk-in help!

Mandy Runnels has worked on political campaigns for ten years in several different states, including Colorado, Florida, Louisiana, Tennessee, and Washington DC. As finance director of the state party, Mandy plans and implements all finance activity, oversees the development of major donor and sustaining membership programs, and coordinates fundraising events across the state.

Why You Should Get Involved in Politics

[by L. C. Baker]

When I stop and think about it, my involvement in the writing of a book on politics is ironic to the point of embarrassment. The truth is that I never cared much for politics. Actually, that's an understatement—the truth is that for most of my life, I've hated politics. I think I could count on one hand the number of times I've voted in my entire life. I was at least twenty-two years old by the time I realized elections were held every year, not just in presidential election years. My apathy probably had something to do with the fact that my mother was so concerned about politics—or rather so concerned about the one issue she cared about, which was such an emotional one for her that we actually left our church when the pastor wouldn't let her put a political display in the narthex. In a typical youthful rejection of the things I felt my parents cared "too much" about, I usually stayed home on voting day, excusing my laziness with the statement that "not voting is my vote: I don't want to support any of the candidates, so I'm voting against all of them."

I never could understand my mother's passion for changing laws or getting "her" politicians elected. To me, they were all the same: dishonest, sleazy, and untrustworthy people who said what people wanted to hear because they were hungry for power. How could a person possibly trust anyone who actually *wanted* to be a politician? I believed firmly that politics held no answers for the problems in our community. What did politics have to say to the pictures I saw on television of children starving to death in Ethiopia? What did politics have to say to the homeless men I saw on the street asking for money or food? What did politics have to say to my friend who was raped when she was fifteen? In my mind, these issues could be impacted only by individuals, by people willing to reach out to another who was hurting, one person at a time.

So how on earth did I end up helping to write a book about politics?

For me, it took living in another country a quarter of the way around the world to realize that politics might be able to make a difference. I spent a year as a missionary in Romania, working with an adventure education and service learning organization for teens called New Horizons Foundation. The goal of NHF is to "create caring citizens who feel empowered to act." If I'd thought about it more before I left, I might have realized that probably indicated some kind of political involvement, but at the time I was so enamored with the idea of living in Romania that I didn't worry so much about what I was actually going to be doing.

Besides, I was extremely interested in service learning. In my mind, service learning meant, well, service projects: picking up trash and running community programs for little kids — that kind of thing. I *love* that kind of thing, so I was even more thrilled at the prospect of doing it in a foreign country.

But it didn't take me long to realize that service learning means a whole lot more than that. The director of the program, Dana Bates, was always urging us to encourage the kids in our service learning clubs to start advocacy projects. He taught us in staff meetings about the different levels of service: direct [when you yourself do the service, such as picking up trash in the park], indirect [when you get lots of groups involved in doing it, like sponsoring a trash pick-up day at all the schools in the city], and advocacy [when you educate people about a need or get laws passed to help a need, such as teaching people not to litter or passing a law that every park needs to have a trash person]. As soon as I stopped to really think about it, the truth that Dana was always trying to convince us of became obvious to me: The last level, the advocacy level, has a much bigger impact. If you pick up trash in the park, then there'll be no trash for a couple of hours. If you get a law passed that the city has to hire a trash person, then someone will be picking up trash every day. And if you educate people about the effects of pollution, then maybe there will be a lot less trash to begin with.

But for me, this experiment of advocacy was still just that: an experiment. The whole idea was something I held at a distance. I had come to Romania to help make it a better place; I was willing to use any means for that. I didn't really need to consider how effective those means were.

But for the kids I was working with, it was more than an experiment: It was a new way of life. I'll never forget the moment when I realized that their need to change things was real and that it had real consequences for them. Most of the youth in Romania want to leave the country; they want to come to America. And when I saw the way life is there, it was hard to blame them. In much of Eastern Europe, corruption is a way of life on every level of society. To ride on the train, you have to slip the conductor some cash. To go to the doctor, you have to bring a present. If you ask most Romanian teens how to succeed in life, their response will include something about lying, cheating, and stealing. It's just the way things are. *Asta este*, as they say in Romanian: "That's the way it is."

But in our service learning clubs, I watched as teens changed their minds about their own country. One day in one of our meetings, the students were talking about America [as they often did when I was around]. Some of them were asking me questions with that dreamy expression they often got when they listened to me talk about a place they pictured as the promised land. Many of them had siblings who had gone to America or to other countries in the West—some of whom they'd never heard from again. But one girl suddenly piped up with words that startled all of us.

"I don't want to go to America," she said, and everyone turned to look at her in surprise.

"Why not?" asked one of the boys. "I'd love to go to America." He grinned at me.

The girl was adamant. "I don't want to run away," she said. "I believe I'm here for a reason. I want to make life better here, in Romania."

We all knew that she had her work cut out for her. She'll spend her life teaching people why they should care, how they can participate in democracy, how to resist corruption, and why they shouldn't litter. But that was the moment when I realized that this was real for these kids. It wasn't just something they were doing for fun; they *had* to change their world because the way it was then was unlivable. But they were determined to do it, and they believed it could be done. And as I watched them writing letters to the mayor and planning presentations to the city council about the safety of children's parks, I realized that I was the one who was running away. I was trying to teach these youth how to change their society when I had never really tried to change mine.

To tell the truth, that's the reason I came back from Romania. I realized I had more to learn there than I had to teach. And if I was going to apply what I'd learned, then I'd have to come back to my home — I'd have to be just like that girl in my club who was willing to work to make her own home a better place.

Since I came back to the U.S., and especially since I moved to downtown Atlanta a few weeks ago, the problems in our society have daily become more obvious to me. As I was biking to the grocery store the other day, I watched two men complete a drug deal on the other side of the street. Last night as I was sitting on my couch and reading, the silence was broken by the sound of an ambulance siren — probably on its way to the prostitution house just blocks from my apartment. And today at the library, as I was registering to vote, a man came to the counter and asked if he could get a library card.

"You just need a Fulton County address," said the librarian.

"Oh, I need an address?" There was a note of desperation in the man's voice.

"Yes, a Fulton County address," the librarian repeated.

"A post office box won't work?"

The librarian shook her head, and the man turned quickly and walked away, defeated. It started me thinking about how much our society discriminates against the homeless. Obviously he can't register to vote, as I was doing just then—he can't even get a library card. But he's a citizen of this country, and the fact that he doesn't have an address right now doesn't make him any less so. Or it shouldn't.

 **I THINK IT'S TIME I WRITE SOME LETTERS TO MY REPRESENTATIVE.**

Final Thought

As you know, people get involved in politics for two reasons: They either desire to bring about change, or they hope to ensure that things stay the same. This is true for any party member. It doesn't matter if you're Republican, Democrat, Green, or independent, each of us enjoys aspects of America's culture that we wouldn't trade for the world, but we also each have a desire to see certain aspects of our culture change dramatically. That's often an interesting and frustrating path to walk—somewhere between desiring a good future for our country and not wanting to limit another's rights.

Some believe politics is the answer to making that path brighter and more peaceful. Eh, well, those people might want to get their heads out of the sand. Politics isn't *the* answer to America's issues; it certainly provides an opportunity to make a few things better, easier, and less expensive, but it's not the answer.

There was a time in my life when I, too, believed politics was the answer for most of America's problems. I thought my goal as a Christian was to ensure that biblical principles remained the core value system in America's government. And sadly, I tried making this a reality through how I voted. But laws and guidelines do not affect the hearts of people. Consequently, even when my partnership with the Christian Coalition was successful at electing the *right* politicians into office and those people made what I believed to be godly decisions, the "heart" of America didn't really change; only the laws changed. Why? Because laws don't change people.

That was a frustrating lesson, but also a freeing one.

You see, it's not the job of people of faith to make sure our government becomes Christianized. That's not the role of politics, nor is it the role of those who follow Jesus. Our goal should be to aid and assist people in government by mercifully educating them on how Jesus wants us to live. If they listen, that's great. If they don't, we go back to doing what *we're* called to do: being concerned for the needy, the homeless, and others society resists; looking out for the environment; and protecting the unborn through ministry. Our politics should simply be one way—maybe not even a huge way—we make these things happen.

Now, you might be thinking, *How should a follower of Jesus deal with politics?* Be informed. Vote your conscience. Resist being divisive with your point of view. Seek out ways to engage the less fortunate. Pay your taxes. And live peaceably. My gosh, *please* live peaceably.

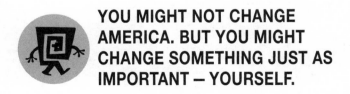

YOU MIGHT NOT CHANGE AMERICA. BUT YOU MIGHT CHANGE SOMETHING JUST AS IMPORTANT — YOURSELF.

[just kidding]

Notes

Political Jeopardy

1. Geoffrey Dickens, "Lauer Offended by Ann Coulter; Delighted by Al Franken," *NewsBusters*, June 6, 2006, http://newsbusters.org/node/5701.

Introduction: The Strange and Complicated World of Politics

1. "Andrew Jackson," http://www.whitehouse.gov/history/presidents/aj7.html.
2. Mary Bellis, "Teddy Roosevelt and the Teddy Bear," *History of the Teddy Bear*, http://inventors.about.com/od/tstartinventions/a/Teddy_Bear.htm.
3. David Maiden, "John F. Kennedy," *Spectrum Home and School Network*, http://www.incwell.com/Biographies/Presidents/Kennedy,JohnF.html.
4. Kelly Holder, "Voting and Registration in the Election of November 2004: Population Characteristics," *U.S. Census Bureau*, March 2006, http://www.census.gov/prod/2006pubs/p20-556.pdf.

Section One: What You Need to Know About the Basics of Politics in America

1. "The Republic of Cascadia," http://republic-of-cascadia.tripod.com/.
2. Franklin Steiner, *The Religious Beliefs of Our Presidents* (1936). See http://www.virginiaplaces.org/religion/religiongw.html.
3. Jerry Falwell, "Falwell vs. Jefferson," *WorldNetDaily Exclusive Commentary*, April 20, 2002, http://www.worldnetdaily.com/news/article.asp?ARTICLE_ID=27316.
4. Each of the previous facts was taken from Oak Hill Publishing Company, "Fascinating Facts About the U.S. Constitution," *U.S. Constitution and Amendments*, http://www.constitutionfacts.com/constitution/Const_facts.htm.
5. Oak Hill Publishing Company, "Proposed Amendments," *U.S. Constitution and Amendments*, http://www.constitutionfacts.com/constitution/proposed.htm.
6. "Democracy vs. Republic," *World Newsstand*, 1999, http://www.wealth4freedom.com/truth/13/DEMvsREPUB.htm.
7. All facts in these lists taken from American Bar Association Division for Media Relations and Public Affairs, *Facts About the American Judicial System*, 1999, http://www.abanet.org/media/factbooks/judifact.pdf. Reprinted by permission from *Facts About the American Judicial System*. Copyright ©1999 American Bar Association. All rights reserved.

Section Two: Politics, the Bible, and Christianity

1. Berit Kjos, "Tolkien's Lord of the Rings: True, Myth or Both?" December 2001, http://www.crossroad.to/articles2/rings.htm#truemyth.
2. Orson Scott Card, *Pastwatch: The Redemption of Christopher Columbus* (New York: Tor, 1996), 78–79.

3. D. D. Webster, "Liberation Theology," http://aibi.gospelcom.net/politics/2/ Liberation%20Theology.pdf, 3–4.

Section Three: The Issues

1. "Active State Medical Marijuana Programs," *NORML*, December 1, 2004, http://www.norml.org/index.cfm?Group_ID=3391.
2. National Center for Health Statistics, "Illegal Drug Use," *Fast Stats A to Z*, http://www.cdc.gov/nchs/fastats/druguse.htm.
3. Public Agenda, "Which Drugs People Use," *Illegal Drugs: Fact File*, 2006, http://www.publicagenda.org/issues/factfiles_detail.cfm?issue_type=illegal _drugs&list=1. Cited from Substance Abuse and Mental Health Services Administration, "2003 National Survey on Drug Use and Health," September 2004.
4. *Wikipedia*, s.v. "War on Drugs," http://en.wikipedia.org/wiki/War_on_Drugs (accessed November 10, 2006).
5. Public Agenda, "Number of Drug Arrests," *Illegal Drugs: Fact File*, 2006, http://www.publicagenda.org/issues/factfiles_detail.cfm?issue_type=illegal _drugs&list=9. Cited from Federal Bureau of Investigation, "Estimated Drug Abuse Violations Arrests, 1979-2002."
6. Paige M. Harrison and Allen J. Beck, PhD, "Prisoners in 2004," *Bureau of Justice Statistics Bulletin*, October 2005, http://www.ojp.usdoj.gov/bjs/pub/pdf/p04.pdf.
7. Amnesty International, "Facts and Figures on the Death Penalty," http://web.amnesty.org/pages/deathpenalty-facts-eng.
8. Gun Owners Foundation, "Gun Control Fact-Sheet," March 2004, http://www.gunowners.org/fs0404.htm.
9. Brady Campaign to Prevent Gun Violence, "Fact Sheets," http://www.bradycampaign.org/facts/factsheets/.
10. A. Dean Byrd and Stony Olsen, "Homosexuality: Innate and Immutable?" *Regent University Law Review* 14:513 (2002), http://www.regent .edu/acad/schlaw/academics/lawreview/articles/14_2Byrd.pdf.
11. The National Law Center on Homelessness and Poverty, "Homelessness in the United States and the Human Right to Housing."
12. General Convention, *Journal of the General Convention of . . . The Episcopal Church, Indianapolis, 1994* (New York: General Convention, 1995), 323–325. Also available at http://www.episcopalarchives.org/cgi-bin/acts_new/acts _resolution-complete.pl?resolution=1994-A054.
13. Presbyterian Church (USA), *Minutes of the 204th General Assembly*, 1992. Also available at http://www.pcusa.org/101/101-abortion.htm.
14. The United Methodist Church, *The Book of Discipline of the United Methodist Church* (The United Methodist Publishing House, 2004). Also available at http://archives.umc.org/interior.asp?mid=1732.
15. *Encarta World English Dictionary*, Microsoft Corporation, 1999, s.v. "Isolationism."
16. Thomson Nelson, "Glossary and Definitions," http://www.kirton.nelson. com/student/glossary.html#u. For more information about the UN, see www.

un.org.
17. Americans for Immigration Control, Inc., "Mexicans Say Southwest U.S. Belongs to Them: Shouldn't Need Permission to Enter U.S.," June 11, 2002, http://www.immigrationcontrol.com/AIC_Zogby_Mexican_Poll.htm.
18. Marv Wegner, "It's Not Easy Being Green & Christian," *The Plain Truth*, January/February 2006, 6.

Section Four: How *You* Get Involved

1. Montgomery County Republican Party, "About the Republican Party: History," http://www.mcgop.net/History.htm.
2. "The Democratic Donkey and the Republican Elephant," *Fact Monster*, http://www.factmonster.com/ipka/A0881985.html.
3. "Party History," *The Democratic Party*, http://www.democrats.org/a/party/history.html.
4. "The Democratic Donkey and the Republican Elephant."

About the Authors

MATTHEW PAUL TURNER is the best-selling author of *The Christian Culture Survival Guide* and *Provocative Faith*. Before he began speaking and writing full-time, he served as editor of *CCM* and music and entertainment editor for Crosswalk.com. He and his wife, Jessica, live in Nashville, Tennessee. To find out more about Matthew, visit his website at www.MatthewPaulTurner.com.

L. C. BAKER is a freelance writer, musician, and youth minister who has published articles in *CCM*, Crosswalk.com, and *HomeLife* magazine. She is also the book section editor for HollywoodJesus.com. In her spare time, she volunteers with several political groups, reads incessantly, and works in a community garden. She lives in Atlanta with her husband, Matt, and their absurdly large collection of books.

"Right now, all over the world, the child relief organization World Vision is helping to save the lives of millions of children. Whether a country is crazed with famine, or by AIDS or by natural disaster, World Vision is there reaching out to individuals and communities with things like physical, emotional and spiritual help. World Vision continues to be the hands and feet of Jesus throughout the world."

— Matthew Paul Turner